SPIRITS OF THE SOMME

EDITED AND INTRODUCED BY
BOB CARRUTHERS

Pen & Sword
MILITARY

This edition published in 2014 by

Pen & Sword Military
An imprint of
Pen & Sword Books Ltd
47 Church Street
Barnsley
South Yorkshire
S70 2AS

ISBN: 9781473822757

A CIP catalogue record for this book is available from the British Library

Printed and bound in England
By CPI Group (UK) Ltd, Croydon, CR0 4YY

Pen & Sword Books Ltd incorporates the imprints of Pen & Sword Aviation, Pen & Sword Family
History, Pen & Sword Maritime, Pen & Sword Military, Pen & Sword Discovery, Pen & Sword
Politics, Pen & Sword Atlas, Pen & Sword Archaeology, Wharncliffe Local History, Wharncliffe
True Crime, Wharncliffe Transport, Pen & Sword Select, Pen & Sword Military Classics, Leo
Cooper, The Praetorian Press, Claymore Press, Remember When, Seaforth Publishing and
Frontline Publishing

For a complete list of Pen & Sword titles please contact
PEN & SWORD BOOKS LIMITED
47 Church Street, Barnsley, South Yorkshire, S70 2AS, England
E-mail: enquiries@pen-and-sword. co. uk
Website: www. pen-and-sword. co. uk

CONTENTS

INTRODUCTION

by Bob Carruthers

THE REMARKABLE PHOTOGRAPHS OF THE Battle of the Somme, and those scenes which were shot for the official film of the Battle of the Somme by Geoffrey Malins and John McDowell have gone on to become iconic images which capture the essence of the Great War. Those images were filmed and photographed in late June and early July 1916 and it is those surviving images of the Great War, more so than any others, which have come to define our perceptions of the war in the trenches. They provide a gritty and compelling primary source record of those terrible events as they unfolded.

Today many of the men who look back at us from almost a century ago are still there, they lie in the dozens of military cemeteries which grace the landscape of the Picardy region in Northern France. The triumphs and disasters which befell the men of the British Fourth army were also observed and brilliantly recorded by Official War Correspondent Sir Philip Gibbs. Gibbs laboured under the burden of censorship during the Great War itself, but shortly after the war, once he was freed from the shackles of officialdom, he published a hard hitting and candid account of the war entitled *Now It Can be Told*. This excellent but often overlooked account provides a vivid primary source from the perspective of a man who was a trained writer and observer. Gibbs was an eyewitness to many of the key events of the Battle of the Somme and he also had access to those in command as well as those fighting in the trenches.

Over one million men from both sides were killed or wounded in the fields and towns of Picardy and the work of Gibbs and Malins stands as an enduring testament to their experience. However Gibbs and Malins can only ever tell part of the story, to complete the picture we need to hear the testimony of those who actually fought on the Somme. We are fortunate therefore to have a large number of accounts left to us by the participants in the battle to draw upon.

When I was invited to make my own film of the events of 1st July 1916 I wanted to contrast the experience of the men who served in 1916 with the work which is being done on the battlefield today to honour the memory of the one million who fought and died there. Once work began in earnest on the film I was spurred to revisit the work of both Malins and Gibbs.

As a result of reviewing the Battle of the Somme film and once more and also reading Gibbs' wonderfully evocative account of the battle in *Now It Can Be Told*, I decided that I would take up the offer to make the film, and as a result I would once more return to those fields and villages which occupy such a unique place in British military history. I am pleased to say that the resulting film which finally emerged (also entitled *Spirits of the Somme*) was well enough received to encourage my publishers at Pen and Sword to ask me to put together the book you now hold.

Approaching the book I felt it was important to let the voices of those who fought on the Somme or who witnessed those tragic events at first hand speak for themselves. Faced with the powerful authority of the eyewitness there is little that the modern historian can add other than to set the sources in context. I was keen to show the battle from as many perspectives as possible without reducing those invaluable accounts to mere snippets. I have therefore chosen six primary source accounts in an attempt to show the battle from the perspective of, not just the front line soldier, but also the artillerymen who played such a major role in the battle. There are surprisingly few books in print which describe the battle from the point of view if the artillery. For that reason I have included an extract from C. A. Rose's account of a field battery in action on the Somme.

I still feel that the work of Sir Philip Gibbs is among the finest observations of the men who fought on the Somme and in my opinion it is an invaluable source as he met everyone from the top down to the privates in the trenches. Unlike the participants Gibbs had nothing else to distract him from the job of observing and recording. He was a masterful writer and the results speak for themselves.

The film reporters of the day were represented at the battle by Geoffrey Malins and his wonderful published account *How I Filmed the War* provides a vivid record of the key events which Malins and McDowell captured in the official film of the Battle of the Somme.

The 60,000 men of the British and Commonwealth armies who were maimed or wounded are represented by the tragic account of the battle which was written from the perspective of Sir Gilbert Nobbs who lost his sight on 1st July 1916.

I have also included an account by Robert Derby Holmes which provides an highly unusual perspective on the Battle of the Somme. Robert Derby Holmes was an American who volunteered to fight in the ranks of the British Army and saw a great deal of action during the Great War. Like Gilbert Nobbs he later had the misfortune to be wounded but he was able to make a full recovery and produced a highly readable account of his war which was published under the title *A Yankee In the Trenches*.

Finally I have chosen the poignant last letters of Isaac Alexander Mack to represent the 20,000 souls who lost their lives.

I hope this collection brings a new insight into the battle and will spur you on to make your own journey to the battlefield. If you do, I would recommend visiting on 1st July, the day when the 'Spirits of the Somme' can be felt almost palpably.

- CHAPTER 1 -

THE BATTLE THEN AND NOW

by Bob Carruthers

STRATEGICALLY THE BATTLE OF THE SOMME was fought as part of a simultaneous series of offensives in 1916 by the British, French, Italian and Russian armies which designed to place intolerable pressure on the Central Powers and bring the war to a swift end.

On the German side the Chief of the German General Staff, Erich von Falkenhayn also intended to end the war in 1916. He sought to do so by destroying the French army. He planned to do this by luring the French into a battle of attrition over ground of his own choosing.

In February 1916 it was Falkenhayn who stole the initiative and began a massive attack towards Verdun. This was the beginning of the massive battle which was designed to grind down the French army and bleed France dry. Erich von Falkenhayn came very close to achieving his aim, but the battle of attrition at Verdun also depleted the German strategic reserve and reduced the German options on the British sector north of the Somme to a policy of steadfast and unyielding defence.

With the pressure mounting at Verdun, on 16th June 1916, General Sir Douglas Haig commander of the British Expeditionary Force ordered that the long awaited British offensive was to be commenced. The main purpose of the offensive was to relieve pressure on the French at Verdun and inflict as much loss as possible on the thinly stretched German forces.

The attack was to be made by five divisions of the French Sixth Army either side of the Somme and thirteen British divisions of the

British Fourth Army north of the Somme. A further seven divisions of the British third Army were also involved in a diversionary attack at Gommecourt. The hammer blow would fall against the German Second Army led by General Fritz von Below.

The British attack was to be preceded by a massive artillery barrage on a hitherto unheralded scale. 1,500 British and French guns fired over one and a half million shells into the German lines. It was expected to be an artillery bombardment of such unrivalled scale and intensity that not even a rat could survive in the German trenches. On the fifth day the British Fourth Army was expected to rise from its trenches and advance through the shattered German defences and capture sixteen miles of the German first line from Montauban to Serre. Simultaneously the British Third Army was to mount its diversionary attack at Gommecourt. The extensive preparations which were necessary meant that the British attack would not remain secret for long and it came to be known as the "Big Push." It was postponed for two days due to bad weather and finally scheduled for 1st July 1916.

The phrase 'going over the top' came into common usage during the Great war and has entered the language as a byword for ineffective fury. This type of frontal assault was rare but it was being tried on a wide front stretching some seven miles on either side of La Boiselle, the village which lay at the centre of the British attack. The attack on its first day was designed to push the British forces eight miles along the straight Roman road which leads from Albert to Bapaume. It was to prove a catastrophic failure.

The killing machine which took such a heavy toll on the men of the British and Commonwealth forces was based on the almost impregnable German lines of defence. The German trench system on the Western Front represented the western rampart of the new German Empire, there was therefore a marked difference in attitude towards the business on trench warfare. While the British viewed their trenches as a temporary solution the Germans were quite prepared to hold what they had captured.

On the Somme front a highly effective construction plan, devised in

January 1915, had since been completed. As a result the German front line had been strengthened by increasing the number of trench lines from one line to three. Each was set about 200 yards apart, the first trench was lightly held and occupied by sentry groups, the second line was occupied by the main front-trench garrison. The third trench held local reserves.

The German trenches were traversed and had sentry-posts in concrete recesses built into the parapet. Dugouts had been deepened to twenty to thirty feet they were spaced fifty yards apart and large enough for twenty-five men. An intermediate line of strong points (*Stutzpunktlinie*) about 1,000 yards positioned about behind the front line was also built.

Barbed wire obstacles had been enlarged from one belt which was only five to ten yards wide to two, strong belts each thirty yards wide and about fifteen yards apart. Double and triple thickness wire was used and formed into belts three to five feet high.

The German defenders, with meticulous planning had constructed telephone with lines buried six feet deep for five miles behind the front line which were used to connect the front line to the artillery.

German artillery was highly effective organised in a series of *sperrfeuerstreifen* (or barrage sectors); each officer was expected to know the batteries covering his section of the front line and the batteries were constantly ready to engage even the most fleeting targets. Despite their inherent strengths the German defences however had two essential weaknesses which the rebuilding had not remedied.

The German front trenches were invariably located on a forward slope, where they were clearly out- lined by white chalk spoil from the subsoil from which the trenches were excavated and they were therefore easily seen by ground observers. The defending forces were also concentrated towards the front trench which made them vulnerable to artillery fire of all calibres and types including field guns and trench mortars. Although they were accommodated in the new deep dugouts this concentration of troops at the front line on a forward slope, guaranteed that they would face the bulk of the British artillery bombardment which could be easily directed by ground observers on clearly marked lines.

The main problem for the German defenders however was their relative lack of numbers. The thinly stretched Imperial German Army could deploy only two thirds of the strength of their formidable British opponents.

In addition to the massive British artillery barrage other preparations were made including exploding two colossal mines under the German trenches on either side of the village of La Boiselle.

Despite all of the preparations the opening day of the Battle of the Somme was a disaster. On the opening day of the battle on the 1st of July 1916, the British Army suffered what can only be described as a crushing defeat. 60,000 casualties were incurred on that single day and of those some 20,000 men were killed.

The British artillery barrage was not altogether ineffective it had certainly caused extensive casualties which, in some sectors of the German front, ran to around ten percent of the German defenders, but except in a few limited instances in the southern sector it was never going to be enough to achieve what was expected of it.

The men fighting to the north of La Boiselle including the Newfoundlanders at Beaumont Hammel and the famous Ulster Division at Thièpval had advanced in confident expectation that the huge seven day artillery bombardment by 1,500 guns of all calibres would have destroyed the German defences. They were proved wrong. Although the Ulster Division achieved a small measure of success and actually penetrated the German front line trenches.

Many of the men who look into the camera of Geoffrey Malins and wave to us now lie in one of the hundreds of cemeteries which mark the landscape.

To the south of La Boiselle the Gordons and the Devons enjoyed a small measure of success on their southern sector of the front. The village of Mametz was captured after a well-executed assault but at came at a heavy price and many of the men of the Gordons, the Manchesters and the Devons lie in their lonely cemeteries to this day. Along with the twenty other British Divisions who took part in the action on 1st July they are remembered to this day. Every year they are commemorated by dozens of events and ceremonies taking place all over the battlefield which range from informal local events to very sombre formal affairs.

A visit to the battlefield of the Somme is never wasted at any time of year but to travel to the Somme on 1st July is to join a communion with thousands of fellow travellers which adds a special dimension to the power of the events which still call to us from a century ago.

The most formal service on the battlefield on 1st July is the one organised by The Royal British Legion in conjunction with the British Embassy in Paris and the Commonwealth War Graves Commission. It takes place at the Thièpval Memorial to the Missing. There is also a low key commemoration of the German war dead in the village of Fricourt which in a spirit of reconciliation is organised by the local villagers.

In contrast to the formality of the Thièpval memorial service There is an informal and unofficial event at the Lochnagar crater the site of a huge mine explosion near La Boiselle. The mine crater was saved from being filled in by the efforts of Richard Dunning who is responsible for keeping this spectacular relic of the Great War memory alive today.

The huge mine at Lochnagar was the result of one of the most spectacular events on 1st July, but it was merely one aspect of the bitter and clandestine war which was being fought underground just a few hundred yards away at the village of la Boiselle. During the war the men on the western front lived and fought in trenches like those which have recently been rediscovered and excavated at the village of La Boiselle by the dedicated team of historians and archaeologists who make up the La Boiselle study group.

Even today the bodies of those British and French miners who were killed at la Boiselle are still entombed deep underground but we are fortunate to benefit from pioneering work by Simon Jones who has worked to locate the place on the surface which is directly above the spot where the bodies lie and to memorialise their stories. It is fortunate that thanks to the unselfish actions of the La Boiselle group who give their services for free we are continually gaining new insights into the battles which raged underground during the Great War.

On the morning of 1st July British gains were negligible and the losses were colossal. All day a stream of dead and wounded were brought into the dressing stations.

Towards the end of the day the only signs which even hinted at success were the steady trickle of German prisoners who were brought in from the Fricourt/Mametz sector and assembled near the village of Carnoy. Most of the men who look back at us from the Battle of the Somme film are the men of the 109th Reserve Infantry Regiment from Baden a few are from the 23rd Infantry regiment which recruited mainly in Silesia.

The Battle of the Somme raged on for 141 days in total without a major strategic breakthrough or even reaching those objectives which had been designated for capture on the first day.

By the end of the battle The Anglo-French armies had failed to capture Péronne and were still three miles from Bapaume which was supposed to have been captured on the first day.

General Sir Douglas Haig, the commander of the BEF and General Henry Rawlinson commander of the Fourth Army, have been criticised ever since, for the human cost of the battle and for failing to achieve their territorial objectives.

On 1st August 1916 Winston Churchill began the trend with his criticism of the British Army's conduct of the offensive to the British Cabinet. He felt that although the battle had forced the Germans to end their offensive at Verdun, attrition was damaging the British armies more than the German forces facing them.

The opposing view to Churchill's is that Battle of the Somme was actually part of a grand strategy which ultimately proved successful. There are many who argue that the Somme was a vital British contribution towards the strategic objectives of a coalition war and that it was a necessary part of a process which took the strategic initiative from the German Army and caused it irreparable damage, leading to its collapse in late 1918.

Its important to remember that The German defence south of the Albert-Bapaume road mostly collapsed and from the army boundary at Maricourt to the Albert-Bapaume road the British enjoyed significant success.

To the south of the Somme the French also enjoyed considerable success and There is little doubt that Germany could not stand losses on this scale.

The Battle of the Somme should have been a success everything possible was done to make it a success, a huge assembly of stores, supplies was brought together, the troops were in peak fighting condition and the objectives were very clear.

The men were fit healthy fresh and eager for the fight. The British artillery achieved numerical superiority over its German counterparts on the Somme and many German guns and their vital crews were destroyed in the build up to the battle, but it was always a fiercely fought contest as the batteries on both sides were constantly hunted by enemy aircraft ever ready to bring down a torrent of counter-battery fire.

Nonetheless it must be stressed that the German defenders on the commanding ground north of the Albert to Bapaume road inflicted a huge defeat on the British infantry. 1st July 1916 was the worst day in the history of British Army, which reeled under the weight of those 60,000 casualties. Those men were killed and wounded mainly on the front between the Albert-Bapaume road and Gommecourt, where the attack failed disastrously, with few British troops reaching the German front line.

The original British Expeditionary Force which had begun the war in 1914 had lost most of the army's pre-war regular soldiers in the battles of 1914 and 1915. By 1916 The bulk of the army was made up of volunteers of the Territorial Force and Kitchener's New Army, which had begun forming in August 1914.

Much of the army was composed of Pals battalions, recruited from the same places and occupations, the such severe losses focused on a particular area had a profound social impact in Britain.

During the first day of the battle British casualties were so obviously overwhelming that the German defenders allowed several truces to be negotiated, in order to allow stretcher parties to recover wounded from 'No Man's Land' north of the road. By the end of the day The Fourth Army had lost 57,470 casualties, of which 19,240 men were killed, and even the well dug in the German 2nd Army had between 10,000 and 12,000 losses.

The stark truth is that from the Albert-Bapaume road to Gommecourt the British attack was a disaster and in recognition of that fact Haig abandoned the offensive north of the road, to reinforce the success in the south.

At the start of 1916, the British Army had been a largely inexperienced and patchily trained mass of volunteers. The Somme was the debut of the Kitchener Army created by Lord Kitchener's call for recruits at the start of the war. The British volunteers were often the fittest, most enthusiastic and best educated citizens, however the fact is that they were not experienced soldiers. The British casualties were therefore chiefly incurred among inexperienced soldiers and their loss, although tragic in human terms, was of lesser military significance than the losses of the experienced men of the German army whose trained soldiers were becoming irreplaceable.

British survivors of the battle certainly gained experience and the new armies of the contributed to the process by which the BEF learned how to conduct the mass warfare that the other armies had been fighting since 1914. However each casualty and every man taken prisoner sapped the experience and effectiveness of the German army. The destruction of German units in battle was made worse by the dominance of British aircraft and long-range guns which reached well behind the front-line.

After the battle Crown Prince Rupprecht of Bavaria stated: "What remained of the old first-class peace-trained German infantry had been expended on the battlefield".

In the cold light of day it seems that a war of attrition was a logical and effective strategy for Britain to use against Germany which, we must not forget, was also at war with France and Russia. A school of thought holds that the Battle of the Somme placed unprecedented strain on the German Army and that after the battle it was unable to replace casualties like-for-like, which reduced the German army to a "militia".

There was no spectacular gain in terms of ground captured. By the end of the Battle of the Somme in November The British and French advanced about six miles, on a front of sixteen miles at a cost of 419,654 British casualties against an estimated 200,000 German casualties who were lost on the British sector.

At the end of the battle, although British and French forces had penetrated just those six miles into German-occupied territory, they had nonetheless taken more ground than in any offensive since the Battle of the Marne in 1914.

Until the 1930s the dominant view of the battle was that the Somme was a hard-fought victory against a brave, experienced and well-led opponent. However in the 1960s the view changed and the popular conception took hold that the battle was a futile slaughter planned by incompetents took hold. The very name of the battle has become a byword for waste, futility and the debate has lasted for almost one hundred years. The British Generals Haig and Rawlinson have been characterised as stubborn pig headed obstinate and slow to learn.

Coming here on 1st July it's hard not to sympathise with that view, but it is not a view that many historians can agree upon.

In recent years a more nuanced version of the original orthodoxy has arisen which does not seek to minimize the human cost of the battle, but sets it in the context of industrial warfare in which the only long term option was to defeat comparable opponents through a war of exhaustion.

- CHAPTER 2 -

THE BATTLE OF THE SOMME

by Sir Philip Gibbs

SIR PHILIP ARMAND HAMILTON GIBBS (1st May, 1877 - 10th March, 1962) was an English journalist and novelist who served as one of the five official British reporters during the First World War. He was present as a witness to the tragic events of 1st July 1916.

Along with four other men he was officially accredited as a wartime correspondent, his work appearing in the *Daily Telegraph* and *Daily Chronicle*. The price he had to pay for his accreditation was to submit to effective censorship: all of his work was to be vetted by C. E. Montague, formerly of the *Manchester Guardian*. Although unhappy with the arrangement Gibbs had no alternative and agreed to have his work vetted.

Gibbs' wartime output was prodigious. He not only produced a stream of newspaper articles, but also a series of books: *The Soul of the War* (1915), *The Battle of the Somme* (1917), *From Bapaume to Passchendaele* (1918) and *The Realities of War* (1920). In the latter work Gibbs exacted a form of revenge for the frustration he suffered in submitting to wartime censorship; published after the armistice *The Realities of War* painted a most unflattering portrait of Sir Douglas Haig, British Commander-in-Chief in France and Flanders, and his General Headquarters. Gibbs also published *Now It Can Be Told* (1920), an account of his personal experiences in war-torn Europe which was designed to set the record straight once he had been freed from the shackles of censorship.

* * * * *

SCORES OF TIMES, HUNDREDS OF TIMES, during the battles of the Somme, I passed the headquarters of Gen. Sir Henry Rawlinson, commanding the Fourth Army, and several times I met the army commander there and elsewhere. One of my first meetings with him was extraordinarily embarrassing to me for a moment or two. While he was organizing his army, which was to be called, with unconscious irony, "The Army of Pursuit" - the battles of the Somme were a siege rather than a pursuit - he desired to take over the château at Tilques, in which the war correspondents were then quartered. As we were paying for it and liked it, we put up an opposition which was most annoying to his A.D.C.'s, especially to one young gentleman of enormous wealth, haughty manners, and a boyish intolerance of other people's interests, who had looked over our rooms without troubling to knock at the doors, and then said, "This will suit us down to the ground." On my way back from the salient one evening I walked up the drive in the flickering light of summer eve, and saw two officers coming in my direction, one of whom I thought I recognized as an old friend.

"Hullo!" I said, cheerily. "You here again?"

Then I saw that I was face to face with Sir Henry Rawlinson. He must have been surprised, but dug me in the ribs in a genial way, and said, "Hullo, young feller!"

He made no further attempt to "pinch" our quarters, but my familiar method of address could not have produced that result.

His headquarters at Querrieux were in another old château on the Amiens-Albert road, surrounded by pleasant fields through which a stream wound its way. Everywhere the sign-boards were red, and a military policeman, authorised to secure obedience to the rules thereon, slowed down every motor-car on its way through the village, as though Sir Henry Rawlinson lay sick of a fever, so anxious were his gestures and his expression of "Hush! Do be careful!"

The army commander seemed to me to have a roguish eye. He seemed to be thinking to himself, "This war is a rare old joke!" He spoke habitually of the enemy as "the old Hun" or "old Fritz," in an affectionate, contemptuous way, as a fellow who was trying his best but getting the worst of it every time. Before the battles of the Somme I had a talk with him among his maps, and found that I had been to many places in his line which he did not seem to know. He could not find them very quickly on his large-sized maps, or pretended not to, though I concluded that this was "camouflage," in case I might tell "old Fritz" that such places existed. Like most of our generals, he had amazing, overweening optimism. He had always got the enemy "nearly beat," and he arranged attacks during the Somme fighting with the jovial sense of striking another blow which would lead this time to stupendous results. In the early days, in command of the 7th Division, he had done well, and he was a gallant soldier, with initiative and courage of decision and a quick intelligence in open warfare. His trouble on the Somme was that the enemy did not permit open warfare, but made a siege of it, with defensive lines all the way back to Bapaume, and every hillock a machine-gun fortress and every wood a death-trap. We were always preparing for a "break-through" for cavalry pursuit, and the cavalry were always being massed behind the lines and then turned back again, after futile waiting, encumbering the roads. "The blood bath of the Somme," as the Germans called it, was ours as well as theirs, and scores of times when I saw the dead bodies of our men lying strewn over those dreadful fields, after desperate and, in the end, successful attacks through the woods of death - Mametz Wood, Delville Wood, Trones Wood, Bernafay Wood, High Wood, and over the Pozières ridge to Courcellette and Martinpuich - I thought of Rawlinson in his château in Querrieux, scheming out the battles and ordering up new masses of troops to the great assault over the bodies of their dead… Well, it is not for generals to sit down with their heads in their hands, bemoaning slaughter, or to shed tears over their maps when directing battle. It is their job to be cheerful, to harden their hearts against the casualty lists, to keep out of the danger-zone unless their presence is strictly necessary. But it is inevitable that the men who risk death daily, the fighting-men who carry out the plans of the High Command and see no sense in them, should be savage in their irony when they pass a peaceful house where their doom is being planned, and green-eyed when they see an army general taking a stroll in buttercup fields, with a jaunty young A.D.C. slashing the flowers with his cane and telling the latest joke from London to his laughing chief. As onlookers of sacrifice some of us - I, for one - adopted the point of view of the men who were to die, finding some reason in their hatred of the staffs, though they were doing their job with a sense of duty, and with as much intelligence as God had given them. Gen. Sir Henry Rawlinson was one of our best generals, as may be seen by the ribbons on his breast, and in the last phase commanded a real "Army of Pursuit," which had the enemy on the run, and broke through to victory. It was in that last phase of open warfare that Rawlinson showed his qualities of generalship and once again that driving purpose which was his in the Somme battles, but achieved only by prodigious cost of life.

*   *   *   *   *

Of General Allenby, commanding the Third Army before he was succeeded by Gen. Sir Julian Byng and went to his triumph in Palestine, I knew very little except by hearsay. He went by the name of "The Bull," because of his burly size and deep voice. The costly fighting that followed the Battle of Arras on April 9th along the *glacis* of the Scarpe did not reveal high generalship. There were many young officers - and some divisional generals - who complained bitterly of attacks ordered without sufficient forethought, and the stream of casualties which poured back, day by day, with tales of tragic happenings did not inspire one with a sense of some high purpose behind it all, or some presiding genius.

General Byng, "Bungo Byng," as he was called by his troops, won the admiration of the Canadian Corps which he commanded, and afterward, in the Cambrai advance of November, 1917, he showed daring of conception and gained the first striking surprise in the war by novel methods of attack - spoiled by the quick come-back of the enemy under Von Marwitz and our withdrawal from Bourlon Wood, Masnieres, and Marcoing, and other places, after desperate fighting.

His chief of staff, Gen. Louis Vaughan, was a charming, gentle-mannered man, with a scientific outlook on the problems of war, and so kind in his expression and character that it seemed impossible that he could devise methods of killing Germans in a wholesale way. He was like an Oxford professor of history discoursing on the Marlborough wars, though when I saw him many times outside the Third Army headquarters, in a railway carriage, somewhere near Villers Carbonnel on the Somme battlefields, he was explaining his preparations and strategy for actions to be fought next day which would be of bloody consequence to our men and the enemy.

General Birdwood, commanding the Australian Corps, and afterward the Fifth Army in succession to General Gough, was always known as "Birdie" by high and low, and this dapper man, so neat, so bright, so brisk, had a human touch with him which won him the affection of all his troops.

Gen. Hunter Weston, of the 8th Corps, was another man of character in high command. He spoke of himself in the House of Commons one day as "a plain, blunt soldier," and the army roared with laughter from end to end. There was nothing plain or blunt about him. He was a man of airy imagination and a wide range of knowledge, and theories on life and war which he put forward with dramatic eloquence.

It was of Gen. Hunter Weston that the story was told about the drunken soldier put onto a stretcher and covered with a blanket, to get him out of the way when the army commander made a visit to the lines.

"What's this?" said the general.

"Casualty, sir," said the quaking platoon commander.

"Not bad, I hope?"

"Dead, sir," said the subaltern. He meant dead drunk.

The general drew himself up, and said, in his dramatic way, "The army commander salutes the honoured dead!"

And the drunken private put his head from under the blanket and asked, "What's the old geezer a-sayin' of?"

That story may have been invented in a battalion mess, but it went through the army affixed to the name of Hunter Weston, and seemed to fit him.

The 8ᵗʰ Corps was on the left in the first attack on the Somme, when many of our divisions were cut to pieces in the attempt to break the German line at Gommecourt. It was a ghastly tragedy, which spoiled the success on the right at Fricourt and Montauban. But Gen. Hunter Weston was not *dégommé* as the French would say, and continued to air his theories on life and warfare until the day of victory, when once again we had "muddled through," not by great generalship, but by the courage of common men.

Among the divisional generals with whom I came in contact - I met most of them at one time or another - were General Hull of the 56ᵗʰ (London) Division, General Hickey of the 16ᵗʰ (Irish) Division, General Harper of the 51ˢᵗ (Highland) Division, General Nugent of the 36ᵗʰ (Ulster) Division, and General Pinnie of the 35ᵗʰ (Bantams) Division, afterward of the 33ʳᵈ.

General Hull was a handsome, straight-speaking, straight-thinking man, and I should say an able general. "Ruthless," his men said, but this was a war of ruthlessness, because life was cheap. Bitter he was at times, because he had to order his men to do things which he knew were folly. I remember sitting on the window-sill of his bedroom, in an old house of Arras, while he gave me an account of "the battle in the dark," in which the Londoners and other English troops lost their direction and found themselves at dawn with the enemy behind them. General Hull made no secret of the tragedy or the stupidity... On another day I met him somewhere on the other side of Péronne, before March 21ˢᵗ, when he was commanding the 16ᵗʰ (Irish) Division in the absence of General Hickey, who was ill. He talked a good deal about the belief in a great German offensive, and gave many reasons for thinking it was all "bluff". A few days later the enemy had rolled over his lines... Out of thirteen generals I met at that time, there were only three who believed that the enemy would make his great assault in a final effort to gain decisive victory, though our Intelligence had amassed innumerable proofs and were utterly convinced of the approaching menace.

"They will never risk it!" said General Gorringe of the 47ᵗʰ (London) Division. "Our lines are too strong. We should mow them down."

I was standing with him on a wagon, watching the sports of the London men. We could see the German lines, south of St.-Quentin, very quiet over there, without any sign of coming trouble. A few days later the place where we were standing was under waves of German storm-troops.

I liked the love of General Hickey for his Irish division. An Irishman himself, with a touch of the old Irish soldier as drawn by Charles Lever, gay-hearted, proud of his boys, he was always pleased to see me because he knew I had a warm spot in my heart for the Irish troops. He had a good story to tell every time, and passed me on to "the boys" to get at the heart of them. It was long before he lost hope of keeping the division together, though it was hard to get recruits and losses were high at Guillemont and Ginchy. For the first time he lost heart and was very sad when the division was cut to pieces in a Flanders battle. It lost 2,000 men and 162 officers before the battle began - they were shelled to death in the trenches - and 2,000 men and 170 officers more during the progress of the battle. It was murderous and ghastly.

General Harper of the 51st (Highland) Division, afterward commanding the 4th Corps, had the respect of his troops, though they called him "Uncle" because of his shock of white hair. The Highland division, under his command, fought many battles and gained great honour, even from the enemy, who feared them and called the kilted men "the ladies from hell." It was to them the Germans sent their message in a small balloon during the retreat from the Somme: "Poor old 51st. Still sticking it! Cheery-oh!"

"Uncle" Harper invited me to lunch in his mess, and was ironical with war correspondents, and censors, and the British public, and new theories of training, and many things in which he saw no sense. There was a smouldering passion in him which glowed in his dark eyes.

He was against bayonet-training, which took the field against rifle-fire for a time.

"No man in this war," he said, with a sweeping assertion, "has ever been killed by the bayonet unless he had his hands up first." And, broadly speaking, I think he was right, in spite of the Director of Training, who was extremely annoyed with me when I quoted this authority.

I met many other generals who were men of ability, energy, high sense of duty, and strong personality. I found them intellectually, with few exceptions, narrowly moulded to the same type, strangely limited in their range of ideas and qualities of character.

"One has to leave many gaps in one's conversation with generals," said a friend of mine, after lunching with an army commander.

That was true. One had to talk to them on the lines of leading articles in *The Morning Post*. Their patriotism, their knowledge of human nature, their idealism, and their imagination were restricted to the traditional views of English country gentlemen of the Tory school. Anything outside that range of thought was to them heresy, treason, or wishy-washy sentiment.

What mainly was wrong with our generalship was the system which put the High Command into the hands of a group of men belonging to the old school of war, unable, by reason of their age and traditions, to get away from rigid methods and to become elastic in face of new conditions.

Our Staff College had been hopelessly inefficient in its system of training, if I am justified in forming such an opinion from specimens produced by it, who had the brains of canaries and the manners of Potsdam. There was also a close corporation among the officers of the Regular Army, so that they took the lion's share of staff appointments, thus keeping out brilliant young men of the new armies, whose brain-power, to say the least of it, was on a higher level than that of the Sandhurst standard. Here and there, where the unprofessional soldier obtained a chance of high command or staff authority, he proved the value of the business mind applied to war, and this was seen very clearly - blindingly - in the able generalship of the Australian Corps, in which most of the commanders, like Generals Hobbs, Monash, and others, were men in civil life before the war. The same thing was observed in the Canadian Corps, General Currie, the corps commander, having been an estate agent, and many of his high officers having had no military training of any scientific importance before they handled their own men in France and Flanders.

*   *   *   *   *

Until 1ˢᵗ July of 1916 the British armies were only getting ready for the big battles which were being planned for them by something greater than generalship - by the fate which decides the doom of men.

The first battles by the Old Contemptibles, down from Mons and up by Ypres, were defensive actions of rear-guards holding the enemy back by a thin wall of living flesh, while behind the New Armies of our race were being raised.

The battles of Festubert, Neuve Chapelle, Loos, were all minor attacks which led to little salients, they were but experimental adventures in the science of slaughter, badly bungled in our laboratories. They had no meaning apart from providing those mistakes by which men learn; ghastly mistakes, burning more than the fingers of life's children. They were only diversions of impatience in the monotonous routine of trench warfare by which our men strengthened the mud walls of their School of Courage, so that the new boys already coming out might learn their lessons without more grievous interruption than came from the daily visits of that Intruder to whom the fees were paid. In those two years it was France which fought the greatest battles, flinging her sons against the enemy's ramparts in desperate, vain attempts to breach them. At Verdun, in the months that followed the first month of 1916, it was France which sustained the full weight of the German offensive on the western front and broke its human waves, until they were spent in a sea of blood, above which the French poilus, the "hairy ones," stood panting and haggard, on their death-strewn rocks. The Germans had failed to deal a fatal blow at the heart of France. France held her head up still, bleeding from many wounds, but defiant still; and the German High Command, aghast at their own losses - six hundred thousand casualties - already conscious, icily, of a dwindling man-power which one day would be cut off at its source, rearranged their order of battle and shifted the balance of their weight eastward, to smash Russia. Somehow or other they must smash a way out by sledge-hammer blows, left and right, west and east, from that ring of nations which girdled them. On the west they would stand now on the defensive, fairly sure of their strength, but well aware that it would be tried to the utmost by that enemy which, at the back of their brains (at the back of the narrow brains of those bald-headed vultures on the German General Staff), they most feared as their future peril - England. They had been fools to let the British armies grow up and wax so strong. It was the folly of the madness by which they had flung the gauntlet down to the souls of proud peoples arrayed against them.

*   *   *   *   *

Our armies were now strong and trained and ready. We had about six hundred thousand bayonet-men in France and Flanders and in England, immense reserves to fill up the gaps that would be made in their ranks before the summer foliage turned to russet tints.

Our power in artillery had grown amazingly since the beginning of the year. Every month I had seen many new batteries arrive, with clean harness and yellow straps, and young gunners who were quick to get their targets. We were strong in "heavies," twelve-inchers, 9.2's, eight- inchers, 4.2's, mostly howitzers, with the long-muzzled sixty-pounders terrible in their long range and destructiveness. Our aircraft had grown fast, squadron upon squadron, and our aviators had been trained in the school of General Trenchard, who sent them out over the German lines to learn how to fight, and how to scout, and how to die like little gentlemen.

For a time our flying-men had gone out on old-fashioned "buses" - primitive machines which were an easy prey to the fast-flying Fokkers who waited for them behind a screen of cloud and then "stooped" on them like hawks sure of their prey. But to the airdrome near St.-Omer came later models, out of date a few weeks after their delivery, replaced by still more powerful types more perfectly equipped for fighting. Our knights-errant of the air were challenging the German champions on equal terms, and beating them back from the lines unless they flew in clusters. There were times when our flying-men gained an absolute supremacy by greater daring - there was nothing they did not dare - and by equal skill. As a rule, and by order, the German pilots flew with more caution, not wasting their strength in unequal contests. It was a sound policy, and enabled them to come back again in force and hold the field for a time by powerful concentrations. But in the battles of the Somme our airmen, at a heavy cost of life, kept the enemy down a while and blinded his eyes.

The planting of new airdromes between Albert and Amiens, the long trail down the roads of lorries packed with wings and the furniture of aircraft factories, gave the hint, to those who had eyes to see, that in this direction a merry hell was being prepared.

There were plain signs of massacre at hand all the way from the coast to the lines. At Etaples and other places near Boulogne hospital huts and tents were growing like mushrooms in the night. From casualty clearing stations near the front the wounded - the human wreckage of routine warfare - were being evacuated "in a hurry" to the base, and from the base to England. They were to be cleared out of the way so that all the wards might be empty for a new population of broken men, in enormous numbers. I went down to see this clearance, this tidying up. There was a sinister suggestion in the solitude that was being made for a multitude that was coming.

"We shall be very busy," said the doctors.

"We must get all the rest we can now," said the nurses.

"In a little while every bed will be filled," said the matrons.

Outside one hut, with the sun on their faces, were four wounded Germans, Würtemburgers and Bavarians, too ill to move just then. Each of them had lost a leg under the surgeon's knife. They were eating strawberries, and seemed at peace. I spoke to one of them.

"Wie befinden sie sich?"

"Ganz wohl; wir sind zufrieden mit unsere behandlung."

I passed through the shell-shock wards and a yard where the "shell-shocks" sat about, dumb, or making queer, foolish noises, or staring with a look of animal fear in their eyes. From a padded room came a sound of singing. Some idiot of war was singing between bursts of laughter. It all seemed so funny to him, that war, so mad!

"We are clearing them out," said the medical officer. "There will be many more soon."

How soon? That was a question nobody could answer. It was the only secret, and even that was known in London, where little ladies in society were naming the date, "in confidence," to men who were directly concerned with it - having, as they knew, only a few more weeks, or days, of certain life. But I believe there were not many officers who would have surrendered deliberately all share in "The Great Push." In spite of all the horror which these young officers knew it would involve, they had to be "in it" and could not endure the thought that all their friends and all their men should be there while they were "out of it." A decent excuse for the safer side of it - yes. A staff job, the Intelligence branch, any post behind the actual shambles - and thank God for the luck. But not an absolute shirk.

Tents were being pitched in many camps of the Somme, rows and rows of bell tents and pavilions stained to a reddish brown. Small cities of them were growing up on the right of the road between Amiens and Albert - at Dernancourt and Daours and Vaux-sous-Corbie. I thought they might be for troops in reserve until I saw large flags hoisted to tall staffs and men of the R.A.M.C. busy painting signs on large sheets stretched out on the grass. It was always the same sign - the Sign of the Cross that was Red.

There was a vast traffic of lorries on the roads, and trains were travelling on light railways day and night to railroads just beyond shell-range. What was all the weight they carried? No need to ask. The "dumps" were being filled, piled up, with row upon row of shells, covered by tarpaulin or brushwood when they were all stacked. Enormous shells, some of them, like gigantic pigs without legs. Those were for the fifteen-inchers, or the 9.2's. There was enough high-explosive force littered along those roads above the Somme to blow cities off the map.

"It does one good to see," said a cheery fellow. "The people at home have been putting their backs into it. Thousands of girls have been packing those things. Well done. Munitions!"

I could take no joy in the sight, only a grim kind of satisfaction that at least when our men attacked they would have a power of artillery behind them. It might help them to smash through to a finish, if that were the only way to end this long-drawn suicide of nations.

My friend was shocked when I said:

"Curse all munitions!"

*   *   *   *   *

The British armies as a whole were not gloomy at the approach of that new phase of war which they called "The Great Push," as though it were to be a glorified football-match. It is difficult, perhaps impossible, to know the thoughts of vast masses of men moved by some sensational adventure. But a man would be a liar if he pretended that British troops went forward to the great attack with hangdog looks or any visible sign of fear in their souls. I think most of them were uplifted by the belief that the old days of trench warfare were over forever and that they would break the enemy's lines by means of that enormous gun-power behind them, and get him "on the run." There would be movement, excitement, triumphant victories - and then the end of the war. In spite of all risks it would be enormously better than the routine of the trenches. They would be getting on with the job instead of standing still and being shot at by invisible earth-men.

"If we once get the Germans in the open we shall go straight through them."

That was the opinion of many young officers at that time, and for once they agreed with their generals.

It seemed to be a question of getting them in the open, and I confess that when I studied the trench maps and saw the enemy's defensive earthworks thirty miles deep in one vast maze of trenches and redoubts and barbed wire and tunnels I was appalled at the task which lay before our men. They did not know what they were being asked to do.

They had not seen, then, those awful maps.

We were at the height and glory of our strength. Out of England had come the flower of our youth, and out of Scotland and Wales and Canada and Australia and New Zealand. Even out of Ireland, with the 16th Division of the south and west, and the 36th of Ulster. The New Armies were made up of all the volunteers who had answered the call to the colours, not waiting for the conscription by class, which followed later. They were the ardent ones, the young men from office, factory, shop, and field, university and public school. The best of our intelligence were there, the noblest of our manhood, the strength of our heart, the beauty of our soul, in those battalions which soon were to be flung into explosive fires.

*   *   *   *   *

In the month of May a new type of manhood was filling the old roads behind the front.

I saw them first in the little old town of St.-Pol, where always there was a coming and going of French and English soldiers. It was market-day and the Grande Place (not very grand) was crowded with booths and old ladies in black, and young girls with checkered aprons over their black frocks, and pigs and clucking fowls. Suddenly the people scattered, and there was a rumble and rattle of wheels as a long line of transport wagons came through the square.

"By Jove!... Australians!"

There was no mistaking them. Their slouch-hats told one at a glance, but without them I should have known. They had a distinctive type of their own, which marked them out from all other soldiers of ours along those roads of war.

They were hatchet-faced fellows who came riding through the little old market town; British unmistakably, yet not English, not Irish, nor Scottish, nor Canadian. They looked hard, with the hardness of a boyhood and a breeding away from cities or, at least, away from the softer training of our way of life. They had merry eyes (especially for the girls round the stalls), but resolute, clean-cut mouths, and they rode their horses with an easy grace in the saddle, as though born to riding, and drove their wagons with a recklessness among the little booths that was justified by half an inch between an iron axle and an old woman's table of coloured ribbons.

Those clean-shaven, sun-tanned, dust-covered men, who had come out of the hell of the Dardanelles and the burning drought of Egyptian sands, looked wonderfully fresh in France. Youth, keen as steel, with a flash in the eyes, with an utter carelessness of any peril ahead, came riding down the street.

They were glad to be there. Everything was new and good to them (though so old and stale to many of us), and after their adventures in the East they found it splendid to be in a civilized country, with water in the sky and in the fields, with green trees about them, and flowers in the grass, and white people who were friendly.

When they came up in the train from Marseilles they were all at the windows, drinking in the look of the French landscape, and one of their officers told me that again and again he heard the same words spoken by those lads of his.

"It's a good country to fight for... It's like being home again."

At first they felt chilly in France, for the weather had been bad for them during the first weeks in April, when the wind had blown cold and rain-clouds had broken into sharp squalls.

Talking to the men, I saw them shiver a little and heard their teeth chatter, but they said they liked a moist climate with a bite in the wind, after all the blaze and glare of the Egyptian sun.

One of their pleasures in being there was the opportunity of buying sweets! "They can't have too much of them," said one of the officers, and the idea that those hard fellows, whose Homeric fighting qualities had been proved, should be enthusiastic for lollipops seemed to me an amusing touch of character. For tough as they were, and keen as they were, those Australian soldiers were but grown-up children with a wonderful simplicity of youth and the gift of laughter.

I saw them laughing when, for the first time, they tried on the gas-masks which none of us ever left behind when we went near the fighting-line. That horror of war on the western front was new to them.

Poison-gas was not one of the weapons used by the Turks, and the gas-masks seemed a joke to the groups of Australians trying on the headgear in the fields, and changing themselves into obscene spectres… But one man watching them gave a shudder and said, "It's a pity such splendid boys should have to risk this foul way of death." They did not hear his words, and we heard their laughter again.

On that first day of their arrival I stood in a courtyard with a young officer whose grey eyes had a fine, clear light, which showed the spirit of the man, and as we talked he pointed out some of the boys who passed in and out of an old barn. One of them had done fine work on the Peninsula, contemptuous of all risks. Another had gone out under heavy fire to bring in a wounded friend… "Oh, they are great lads!" said the captain of the company. "But now they want to get at the Germans and finish the job quickly. Give them a fair chance and they'll go far."

They went far, from that time to the end, and fought with a simple, terrible courage.

They had none of the discipline imposed upon our men by Regular traditions. They were gipsy fellows, with none but the gipsy law in their hearts, intolerant of restraint, with no respect for rank or caste unless it carried strength with it, difficult to handle behind the lines, quick-tempered, foul-mouthed, primitive men, but lovable, human, generous souls when their bayonets were not red with blood. Their discipline in battle was the best. They wanted to get to a place ahead. They would fight the devils of hell to get there.

The New Zealanders followed them, with rosy cheeks like English boys of Kent, and more gentle manners than the other "Anzacs," and the same courage. They went far, too, and set the pace awhile in the last lap. But that, in the summer of 1916, was far away.

In those last days of June, before the big battles began, the countryside of the Somme valley was filled with splendour. The mustard seed had spread a yellow carpet in many meadows so that they were Fields of the Cloth of Gold, and clumps of red clover grew like flowers of blood. The hedges about the villages of Picardy were white with elderflower and drenched with scent. It was haymaking time and French women and children were tossing the hay on wooden pitchforks during hot days which came between heavy rains. Our men were marching through that beauty, and were conscious of it, I think, and glad of life.

* * * * *

Boulogne was a port through which all our youth passed between England and the long, straight road which led to 'No Man's Land'. The seven-days-leave men were coming back by every tide, and all other leave was cancelled.

New "drafts" were pouring through the port by tens of thousands - all manner of men of all our breed marching in long columns from the quayside, where they had orders yelled at them through megaphones by A.P.M.'s, R.T.O.'s, A.M.L.O.'s, and other blue-tabbed officers who dealt with them as cattle for the slaughter-houses. I watched them landing from the transports which came in so densely crowded with the human freight that the men were wedged together on the decks like herrings in barrels. They crossed from one boat to another to reach the gangways, and one by one, interminably as it seemed, with rifle gripped and pack hunched, and steel hat clattering like a tinker's kettle, came down the inclined plank and lurched ashore. They were English lads from every county; Scots, Irish, Welsh, of every regiment; Australians, New-Zealanders, South Africans, Canadians, West Indians of the Garrison Artillery; Sikhs, Pathans, and Dogras of the Indian Cavalry. Some of them had been sick and there was a greenish pallor on their faces. Most of them were deeply tanned. Many of them stepped on the quayside of France for the first time after months of training, and I could tell those, sometimes, by the furtive look they gave at the crowded scene about them, and by a sudden glint in their eyes, a faint reflection of the emotion that was in them, because this was another stage on their adventure of war, and the drawbridge was down at last between them and the enemy. That was all just that look, and lips tightened now grimly, and the pack hunched higher. Then they fell in by number and marched away, with Red-caps to guard them, across the bridge, into the town of Boulogne and beyond to the great camp near Etaples (and near the hospital, so that German aircraft had a good argument for smashing Red Cross huts), where some of them would wait until somebody said, "You're wanted." They were wanted in droves as soon as the fighting began on the first day of July.

The bun-shops in Boulogne were filled with nurses, V.A.D.'s, all kinds of girls in uniforms which glinted with shoulder-straps and buttons. They ate large quantities of buns at odd hours of mornings and afternoons. Flying-men and officers of all kinds waiting for trains crowded the Folkestone Hotel and restaurants, where they spent two hours over luncheon and three hours over dinner, drinking red wine, talking "shop" - the shop of trench-mortar units, machine-gun sections, cavalry squadrons, air-fighting, gas schools, and anti-gas schools. Regular inhabitants of Boulogne, officers at the base, passed to inner rooms with French ladies of dangerous appearance, and the transients envied them and said: "Those fellows have all the luck! What's their secret.? How do they arrange these cushy jobs?" From open windows came the music of gramophones. Through half-drawn curtains there were glimpses of khaki tunics and Sam Brown belts in juxtaposition with silk blouses and coiled hair and white arms. Opposite the Folkestone there was a park of ambulances driven by "Scottish women," who were always on the move from one part of the town to the other. Motor-cars came hooting with staff-officers, all aglow in red tabs and arm-bands, thirsty for little cocktails after a dusty drive. Everywhere in the streets and on the esplanade there was incessant saluting. The arms of men were never still. It was like the St. Vitus disease. Tommies and Jocks saluted every subaltern with an automatic gesture of convulsive energy. Every subaltern acknowledged these movements and in turn saluted a multitude of majors, colonels, generals. The thing became farcical, a monstrous absurdity of human relationship, yet pleasing to the vanity of men lifted up above the lowest caste. It seemed to me an intensification of the snob instinct in the soul of man. Only the Australians stood out against it, and went by all officers except their own with a careless slouch and a look of "To hell with all that hand wagging."

Seated on high stools in the Folkestone, our young officers clinked their cocktails, and then whispered together.

"When's it coming?"

"In a few days... I'm for the Gommecourt sector"

"Do you think we shall get through.?"

"Not a doubt of it. The cavalry are massing for a great drive. As soon as we make the gap they'll ride into the blue."

"By God!... There'll be some slaughter!"

"I think the old Bosch will crack this time."

"Well, cheerio!"

There was a sense of enormous drama at hand, and the excitement of it in boys' hearts drugged all doubts and fears. It was only the older men, and the introspective, who suffered from the torture of apprehension. Even timid fellows in the ranks were, I imagine, strengthened and exalted by the communal courage of their company or battalion, for courage as well as fear is infectious, and the psychology of the crowd uplifts the individual to immense heights of daring when alone he would be terror-stricken. The public-school spirit of pride in a name and tradition was in each battalion of the New Army, extended later to the division, which became the unit of *esprit de corps*. They must not "let the battalion down." They would do their damnedest to get farther than any other crowd, to bag more prisoners, to gain more "kudos." There was rivalry even among the platoons and the companies. "A" Company would show "B" Company the way to go! Their sergeant-major was a great fellow! Their platoon commanders were fine kids!

In that spirit, as far as I - an outsider - could see and hear, did our battalions of boys march forward to "The Great Push," whistling, singing, jesting, until their lips were dry and their throats parched in the dust, and even the merriest jesters of all were silent under the weight of their packs and rifles. So they moved up day by day through the beauty of that June in France - thousands of men - hundreds of thousands - to the edge of the battlefields of the Somme, where the enemy was entrenched in fortress positions and where already, before the last days of June, gun-fire was flaming over a vast sweep of country.

*　*　*　*　*

On the 1st of July, 1916, began those prodigious battles which only lulled down at times during two and a half years more, when our British armies fought with desperate sacrificial valour beyond all previous reckoning; when the flower of our youth was cast into that furnace month after month, recklessly, with prodigal, spendthrift haste; when those boys were mown down in swaths by machine-guns, blown to bits by shell-fire, gassed in thousands, until all that country became a graveyard; when they went forward to new assaults or fell back in rear-guard actions with a certain knowledge that they had in their first attack no more than one chance in five of escape, next time one chance in four, then one chance in three, one chance in two, and after that no chance at all, on the line of averages, as worked out by their experience of luck. More boys came out to take their places, and more, and more, conscripts following volunteers, younger brothers following elder brothers. Never did they revolt from the orders that came to them. Never a battalion broke into mutiny against inevitable martyrdom. They were obedient to the command above them. Their discipline did not break. However profound was the despair of the individual - and it was, I know, deep as the wells of human tragedy in many hearts - the mass moved as it was directed, backward or forward, this way and that, from one shambles to another, in mud and in blood, with the same massed valour as that which uplifted them before that first day of July with an intensified pride in the fame of their divisions, with a more eager desire for public knowledge of their deeds, with a loathing of war's misery, with a sense of its supreme folly, yet with a refusal in their souls to acknowledge defeat or to stop this side of victory. In each battle there were officers and men who risked death deliberately, and in a kind of ecstasy did acts of superhuman courage; and because of the number of these feats the record of them is monotonous, dull, familiar. The mass followed their

38

lead, and even poor coward-hearts, of whom there were many, as in all armies, had courage enough, as a rule, to get as far as the centre of the fury before their knees gave way or they dropped dead.

Each wave of boyhood that came out from England brought a new mass of physical and spiritual valour as great as that which was spent, and in the end it was an irresistible tide which broke down the last barriers and swept through in a rush to victory - to victory which we gained at the cost of nearly a million dead, and a high sum of living agony, and all our wealth, and a spiritual bankruptcy worse than material loss, so that now England is for a time sick to death and drained of her old pride and power.

*　*　*　*　*

I remember, as though it were yesterday in vividness and a hundred years ago in time, the bombardment which preceded the battles of the Somme. With a group of officers I stood on the high ground above Albert, looking over to Gommecourt and Thièpval and La Boisselle, on the left side of the German salient, and then, by crossing the road, to Fricourt, Mametz, and Montauban on the southern side. From Albert westward past Thièpval Wood ran the little river of the Ancre, and on the German side the ground rose steeply to Usna Hill by La Boisselle, and to Thièpval Château above the wood. It was a formidable defensive position - one fortress girdled by line after line of trenches, and earthwork redoubts, and deep tunnels, and dugouts in which the German troops could live below ground until the moment of attack. The length of our front of assault was about twenty miles round the side of the salient to the village of Bray, on the Somme, where the French joined us and continued the battle.

From where we stood we could see a wide panorama of the German positions, and beyond, now and then, when the smoke of shell-fire drifted, I caught glimpses of green fields and flower patches beyond the trench lines, and church spires beyond the range of guns rising above clumps of trees in summer foliage. Immediately below, in the foreground, was the village of Albert, not much ruined then, with its red-brick church and tower from which there hung, head downward, the Golden Virgin with her Babe outstretched as though as a peace-offering over all this strife. That leaning statue, which I had often passed on the way to the trenches, was now revealed brightly with a golden glamour, as sheets of flame burst through a heavy veil of smoke over the valley. In a field close by some troops were being ticketed with yellow labels fastened to their backs. It was to distinguish them so that artillery observers might know them from the enemy when their turn came to go into the battleground. Something in the sight of those yellow tickets made me feel sick… Away behind, a French farmer was cutting his grass with a long scythe, in steady, sweeping strokes. Only now and then did he stand to look over at the most frightful picture of battle ever seen until then by human eyes. I wondered, and wonder still, what thoughts were passing through that old brain to keep him at his work, quietly, steadily, on the edge of hell. For there, quite close and clear, was hell, of man's making, produced by chemists and scientists, after centuries in search of knowledge. There were the fires of hate, produced out of the passion of humanity after a thousand years of Christendom and of progress in the arts of beauty. There was the devil-worship of our poor, damned human race, where the most civilized nations of the world were on each side of the bonfires. It was worth watching by a human ant.

I remember the noise of our guns as all our batteries took their parts in a vast orchestra of drum-fire. The tumult of the field-guns merged into thunderous waves. Behind me a fifteen-inch - "Grandmother" - fired single strokes, and each one was an enormous shock. Shells were rushing through the air like droves of giant birds with beating wings and with strange wailings. The German lines were in eruption. Their earthworks were being tossed up, and fountains of earth sprang up between columns of smoke, black columns and white, which stood rigid for a few seconds and then sank into the banks of fog. Flames gushed up red and angry, rending those banks of mist with strokes of lightning. In their light I saw trees falling, branches tossed like twigs, black things hurtling through space. In the night before the battle, when that bombardment had lasted several days and nights, the fury was intensified. Red flames darted hither and thither like little red devils as our trench- mortars got to work. Above the slogging of the guns there were louder, earth-shaking noises, and volcanoes of earth and fire spouted as high as the clouds. One convulsion of this kind happened above Usna Hill, with a long, terrifying roar and a monstrous gush of flame.

"What is that?" asked some one.

"It must be the mine we charged at La Boisselle. The biggest that has ever been."

It was a good guess. When, later in the battle, I stood by the crater of that mine and looked into its gulfs I wondered how many Germans had been hurled into eternity when the earth had opened. The grave was big enough for a battalion of men with horses and wagons, below the chalk of the crater's lips. Often on the way to Bapaume I stepped off the road to look into that white gulf, remembering the moment when I saw the gust of flame that rent the earth about it.

*   *   *   *   *

There was the illusion of victory on that first day of the Somme battles, on the right of the line by Fricourt, and it was not until a day or two later that certain awful rumours I had heard from wounded men and officers who had attacked on the left up by Gommecourt, Thièpval, and Serre were confirmed by certain knowledge of tragic disaster on that side of the battle-line.

The illusion of victory, with all the price and pain of it, came to me when I saw the German rockets rising beyond the villages of Mametz and Montauban and our barrage fire lifting to a range beyond the first lines of German trenches, and our support troops moving forward in masses to captured ground. We had broken through! By the heroic assault of our English and Scottish troops - West Yorks, Yorks and Lancs, Lincolns, Durhams, Northumberland Fusiliers, Norfolks and

Berkshires, Liverpools, Manchesters, Gordons, and Royal Scots, all those splendid men I had seen marching to their lines - we had smashed through the ramparts of the German fortress, through that maze of earthworks and tunnels which had appalled me when I saw them on the maps, and over which I had gazed from time to time from our front-line trenches when those places seemed impregnable. I saw crowds of prisoners coming back under escort - fifteen hundred had been counted in the first day - and they had the look of a defeated army. Our lightly wounded men, thousands of them, were shouting and laughing as they came down behind the lines, wearing German caps and helmets. From Amiens civilians straggled out along the roads as far as they were allowed by military police, and waved hands and cheered those boys of ours. *"Vive l'Angleterre!"* cried old men, raising their hats. Old women wept at the sight of those gay wounded (the lightly touched, glad of escape, rejoicing in their luck and in the glory of life which was theirs still) and cried out to them with shrill words of praise and exultation.

"Nous les aurons - les sales Boches! Ah, ils sont foutus, ces bandits! C'est la victoire, grâce à vous, petits soldats anglais!"

Victory! The spirit of victory in the hearts of fighting-men, and of women excited by the sight of those bandaged heads, those bare, brawny arms splashed with blood, those laughing heroes.

It looked like victory (in those days, as war correspondents, we were not so expert in balancing the profit and loss as afterward we became) when I went into Fricourt on the third day of battle, after the last Germans, who had clung on to its ruins, had been cleared out by the Yorkshires and Lincolns of the 21st Division (that division which had been so humiliated at Loos and now was wonderful in courage), and when the Manchesters and Gordons of the 30th Division had captured Montauban and repulsed fierce counter-attacks.

It looked like victory, because of the German dead that lay there in their battered trenches and the filth and stench of death over all that mangled ground, and the enormous destruction wrought by our guns, and the fury of fire which we were still pouring over the enemy's lines from batteries which had moved forward.

I went down flights of steps into German dugouts, astonished by their depth and strength. Our men did not build like this. This German industry was a rebuke to us - yet we had captured their work and the dead bodies of their labourers lay in those dark caverns, killed by our bombers, who had flung down hand-grenades. I drew back from those fat corpses. They looked monstrous, lying there crumpled up, amid a foul litter of clothes, stick-bombs, old boots, and bottles. Groups of dead lay in ditches which had once been trenches, flung into chaos by that bombardment I had seen. They had been bayoneted. I remember one man - an elderly fellow - sitting up with his back to a bit of earth with his hands half raised. He was smiling a little, though he had been stabbed through the belly and was stone dead... Victory!... some of the German dead were young boys, too young to be killed for old men's crimes, and others might have been old or young. One could not tell, because they had no faces, and were just masses of raw flesh in rags and uniforms. Legs and arms lay separate, without any bodies thereabouts.

Outside Montauban there was a heap of our own dead. Young Gordons and Manchesters of the 30th Division, they had been caught by blasts of machine-gun fire - but our dead seemed scarce in the places where I walked.

Victory?... Well, we had gained some ground, and many prisoners, and here and there some guns. But as I stood by Montauban I saw that our line was a sharp salient looped round Mametz village and then dipping sharply southward to Fricourt. O God! Had we only made another salient after all that monstrous effort? To the left there was fury at La Boisselle, where a few broken trees stood black on the sky-line on a chalky ridge. Storms of German shrapnel were bursting there, and machine-guns were firing in spasms. In Contalmaison, round a château which stood high above ruined houses, shells were bursting with thunderclaps - our shells. German gunners in invisible batteries were sweeping our lines with barrage-fire - it roamed up and down this side of Montauban Wood, just ahead of me, and now and then shells smashed among the houses and barns of Fricourt, and over Mametz there was suddenly a hurricane of "hate." Our men were working like ants in those muck heaps, a battalion moved up toward Boisselle. From a ridge above Fricourt, where once I had seen a tall crucifix between two trees, which our men called the "Poodles" a body of men came down and shrapnel burst among them and they fell and disappeared in tall grass. Stretcher-bearers came slowly through Fricourt village with living burdens. Some of them were German soldiers carrying our wounded and their own. Walking wounded hobbled slowly with their arms round each other's shoulders, Germans and English together. A boy in a steel hat stopped me and held up a bloody hand. "A bit of luck!" he said. "I'm off, after eighteen months of it."

German prisoners came down with a few English soldiers as their escort. I saw distant groups of them, and a shell smashed into one group and scattered it. The living ran, leaving their dead. Ambulances driven by daring fellows drove to the far edge of Fricourt, not a healthy place, and loaded up with wounded from a dressing station in a tunnel there.

It was a wonderful picture of war in all its filth and shambles. But was it Victory?... I knew then that it was only a breach in the German bastion, and that on the left, Gommecourt way, there had been black tragedy.

* * * * *

On the left, where the 8th and 10th Corps were directing operations, the assault had been delivered by the 4th, 29th, 36th, 49th, 32nd, 8th, and 56th Divisions.

The positions in front of them were Gommecourt and Beaumont Hamel on the left side of the River Ancre, and Thièpval Wood on the right side of the Ancre leading up to Thièpval Château on the crest of the cliff. These were the hardest positions to attack, because of the rising ground and the immense strength of the enemy's earthworks and tunnelled defences. But our generals were confident that the gun-power at their disposal was sufficient to smash down that defensive system and make an easy way through for the infantry. They were wrong. In spite of that tornado of shell-fire which I had seen tearing up the earth, many tunnels were still unbroken, and out of them came masses of German machine-gunners and riflemen, when our infantry rose from their own trenches on that morning of July 1st.

Our guns had shifted their barrage forward at that moment, farther ahead of the infantry than was afterward allowed, the men being trained to follow close to the lines of bursting shells, trained to expect a number of casualties from their own guns - it needs some training! - in order to secure the general safety gained by keeping the enemy below ground until our bayonets were round his dugouts.

The Germans had been trained, too, to an act of amazing courage. Their discipline, that immense power of discipline which dominates men in the mass, was strong enough to make them obey the order to rush through that barrage of ours, that advancing wall of explosion, and, if they lived through it, to face our men in the open with massed machine-gun fire. So they did; and as English, Irish, Scottish, and Welsh battalions of our assaulting divisions trudged forward over what had been 'No Man's Land', machine-gun bullets sprayed upon them, and they fell like grass to the scythe. Line after line of men followed them, and each line crumpled, and only small groups and single figures, seeking comradeship, hurried forward. German machine-gunners were bayoneted as their thumbs were still pressed to their triggers. In German front-line trenches at the bottom of Thièpval Wood, outside Beaumont Hamel and on the edge of Gommecourt Park, the field-gray men who came out of their dugouts fought fiercely with stick-bombs and rifles, and our officers and men, in places where they had strength enough, clubbed them to death, stuck them with bayonets, and blew their brains out with revolvers at short range. Then those English and Irish and Scottish troops, grievously weak because of all the dead and wounded behind them, struggled through to the second German line, from which there came a still fiercer rattle of machine and rifle-fire. Some of them broke through that line, too, and went ahead in isolated parties across the wild crater land, over chasms and ditches and fallen trees, toward the highest ground, which had been their goal. Nothing was seen of them. They disappeared into clouds of smoke and flame. Gunner observers saw rockets go up in far places - our rockets - showing that outposts had penetrated into the German lines. Runners came back - survivors of many predecessors who had fallen on the way - with scribbled messages from company officers. One came from the Essex and King's Own of the 4th Division, at a place called Pendant Copse, southeast of Serre. "For God's sake send us bombs." It was impossible to send them bombs. No men could get to them through the deep barrage of shell-fire which was between them and our supporting troops. Many tried and died.

The Ulster men went forward toward Beaumont Hamel with a grim valour which was reckless of their losses. Beaumont Hamel was a German fortress. Machine-gun fire raked every yard of the Ulster way. Hundreds of the Irish fell. I met hundreds of them wounded - tall, strong, powerful men, from Queen's Island and Belfast factories, and Tyneside Irish and Tyneside Scots.

"They gave us no chance," said one of them - a sergeant-major. "They just murdered us."

But bunches of them went right into the heart of the German positions, and then found behind them crowds of Germans who had come up out of their tunnels and flung bombs at them. Only a few came back alive in the darkness.

Into Thièpval Wood men of ours smashed their way through the German trenches, not counting those who fell, and killing any German who stood in their way. Inside that wood of dead trees and charred branches they reformed, astonished at the fewness of their numbers. Germans coming up from holes in the earth attacked them, and they held firm and took two hundred prisoners. Other Germans came closing in like wolves, in packs, and to a German officer who said, "Surrender!" our men shouted, "No surrender!" and fought on in Thièpval Wood until most were dead and only a few wounded crawled out to tell that tale.

The Londoners of the 56th Division had no luck at all. Theirs was the worst luck because, by a desperate courage in assault, they did break through the German lines at Gommecourt. Their left was held by the London Rifle Brigade. The Rangers and the Queen Victoria

46

Rifles - the old "Vics" - formed their centre. Their right was made up by the London Scottish, and behind came the Queen's Westminsters and the Kensingtons, who were to advance through their comrades to a farther objective. Across a wide 'No Man's Land' they suffered from the bursting of heavy crumps, and many fell. But they escaped annihilation by machine-gun fire and stormed through the upheaved earth into Gommecourt Park, killing many Germans and sending back batches of prisoners. They had done what they had been asked to do, and started building up barricades of earth and sand-bags, and then found they were in a death-trap. There were no troops on their right or left. They had thrust out into a salient, which presently the enemy saw. The German gunners, with deadly skill, boxed it round with shell-fire, so that the Londoners were inclosed by explosive walls, and then very slowly and carefully drew a line of bursting shells up and down, up and down that captured ground, ravaging its earth anew and smashing the life that crouched there - London life.

I have written elsewhere (in *The Battle of the Somme*) how young officers and small bodies of these London men held the barricades against German attacks while others tried to break a way back through that murderous shell-fire, and how groups of lads who set out on that adventure to their old lines were shattered so that only a few from each group crawled back alive, wounded or unwounded.

At the end of the day the Germans acted with chivalry which I was not allowed to tell at the time. The general of the London Division (Phillip Howell) told me that the enemy sent over a message by a low-flying airplane, proposing a truce while the stretcher-bearers worked, and offering the service of their own men in that work of mercy. This offer was accepted without reference to G.H.Q., and German stretcher-bearers helped to carry our wounded to a point where they could be reached.

Many, in spite of that, remained lying out in 'No Man's Land', some for three or four days and nights. I met one man who lay out there wounded, with a group of comrades more badly hurt than he was, until 6th July. At night he crawled over to the bodies of the dead and took their water-bottles and "iron" rations, and so brought drink and food to his stricken friends. Then at last he made his way through roving shells to our lines and even then asked to lead the stretcher-bearers who volunteered on a search-party for his "pals."

"Physical courage was very common in the war," said a friend of mine who saw nothing of war. "It is proved that physical courage is the commonest quality of mankind, as moral courage is the rarest." But that soldier's courage was spiritual, and there were many like him in the battles of the Somme and in other later battles as tragic as those.

*   *   *   *   *

I have told how, before the "Big Push," as we called the beginning of these battles, little towns of tents were built under the sign of the Red Cross. For a time they were inhabited only by medical officers, nurses, and orderlies, busily getting ready for a sudden invasion, and spending their surplus energy, which seemed inexhaustible, on the decoration of their camps by chalk-lined paths, red crosses painted on canvas or built up in red and white chalk on levelled earth, and flowers planted outside the tents - all very pretty and picturesque in the sunshine and the breezes over the valley of the Somme.

On the morning of battle the doctors, nurses, and orderlies waited for their patients and said, "Now we sha'n't be long!" They were merry and bright with that wonderful cheerfulness which enabled them to face the tragedy of mangled manhood without horror, and almost, it seemed, without pity, because it was their work, and they were there to heal what might be healed. It was with a rush that their first cases came, and the M.O.'s whistled and said, "Ye gods! How many more?" Many more. The tide did not slacken. It became a spate brought down by waves of ambulances. Three thousand wounded came to Daours on the Somme, three thousand to Corbie, thousands to Dernancourt, Heilly, Puchevillers, Toutencourt, and many other "clearing stations."

At Daours the tents were filled to overflowing, until there was no more room. The wounded were laid down on the grass to wait their turn for the surgeon's knife. Some of them crawled over to haycocks and covered themselves with hay and went to sleep, as I saw them sleeping there, like dead men. Here and there shell-shocked boys sat weeping or moaning, and shaking with an ague. Most of the wounded were quiet and did not give any groan or moan. The lightly wounded sat in groups, telling their adventures, cursing the German machine-gunners. Young officers spoke in a different way, and with that sporting spirit which they had learned in public schools praised their enemy.

"The machine-gunners are wonderful fellows - topping. Fight until they're killed. They gave us hell."

Each man among those thousands of wounded had escaped death a dozen times or more by the merest flukes of luck. It was this luck of theirs which they hugged with a kind of laughing excitement.

"It's a marvel I'm here! That shell burst all round me. Killed six of my pals. I've got through with a blighty wound. No bones broken... God! What luck!"

The death of other men did not grieve them. They could not waste this sense of luck in pity. The escape of their own individuality, this possession of life, was a glorious thought. They were alive! What luck! What luck!

* * * * *

We called the hospital at Corbie the "Butcher's Shop." It was in a pretty spot in that little town with a big church whose tall white towers looked down a broad sweep of the Somme, so that for miles they were a landmark behind the battlefields. Behind the lines during those first battles, but later, in 1918, when the enemy came nearly to the gates of Amiens, a stronghold of the Australians, who garrisoned it and sniped pigeons for their pots off the top of the towers, and took no great notice of "whizz-bangs" which broke through the roofs of cottages and barns. It was a safe, snug place in July of '16, but that Butcher's Shop at a corner of the square was not a pretty spot. After a visit there I had to wipe cold sweat from my forehead, and found myself trembling in a queer way. It was the medical officer - a colonel - who called it that name. "This is our Butcher's Shop," he said, cheerily. "Come and have a look at my cases. They're the worst possible; stomach wounds, compound fractures, and all that. We lop off limbs here all day long, and all night. You've no idea!"

I had no idea, but I did not wish to see its reality. The M.O. could not understand my reluctance to see his show. He put it down to my desire to save his time - and explained that he was going the rounds and would take it as a favour if I would walk with him. I yielded weakly, and cursed myself for not taking to flight. Yet, I argued, what men are brave enough to suffer I ought to have the courage to see... I saw and was sickened.

These were the victims of "Victory" and the red fruit of war's harvest-fields. A new batch of "cases" had just arrived. More were being brought in on stretchers. They were laid down in rows on the floor-boards. The colonel bent down to some of them and drew their blankets back, and now and then felt a man's pulse. Most of them were unconscious, breathing with the hard snuffle of dying men. Their skin was already darkening to the death-tint, which is not white. They were all plastered with a gray clay and this mud on their faces was, in some cases, mixed with thick clots of blood, making a hard incrustation from scalp to chin.

"That fellow won't last long," said the M.O. , rising from a stretcher. "Hardly a heart-beat left in him. Sure to die on the operating-table if he gets as far as that... Step back against the wall a minute, will you?"

We flattened ourselves against the passage wall while ambulance - men brought in a line of stretchers. No sound came from most of those bundles under the blankets, but from one came a long, agonizing wail, the cry of an animal in torture.

"Come through the wards," said the colonel. "They're pretty bright, though we could do with more space and light."

In one long, narrow room there were about thirty beds, and in each bed lay a young British soldier, or part of a young British soldier. There was not much left of one of them. Both his legs had been amputated to the thigh, and both his arms to the shoulder-blades.

"Remarkable man, that," said the colonel. "Simply refuses to die. His vitality is so tremendous that it is putting up a terrific fight against mortality… There's another case of the same kind; one leg gone and the other going, and one arm. Deliberate refusal to give in. 'You're not going to kill me, doctor,' he said. 'I'm going to stick it through.' What spirit, eh?"

I spoke to that man. He was quite conscious, with bright eyes. His right leg was uncovered, and supported on a board hung from the ceiling. Its flesh was like that of a chicken badly carved - white, flabby, and in tatters. He thought I was a surgeon, and spoke to me pleadingly:

"I guess you can save that leg, sir. It's doing fine. I should hate to lose it."

I murmured something about a chance for it, and the M.O. broke in cheerfully.

"You won't lose it if I can help it. How's your pulse?"

"… Oh, not bad. Keep cheerful and we'll pull you through."

The man smiled gallantly.

"Bound to come off," said the doctor as we passed to another bed. "Gas gangrene. That's the thing that does us down."

In bed after bed I saw men of ours, very young men, who had been lopped of limbs a few hours ago or a few minutes, some of them unconscious, some of them strangely and terribly conscious, with a look in their eyes as though staring at the death which sat near to them, and edged nearer.

"Yes," said the M.O., "they look bad, some of 'em, but youth is on their side. I dare say seventy- five per cent, will get through. If it wasn't for gas gangrene ——"

He jerked his head to a boy sitting up in bed, smiling at the nurse who felt his pulse.

"Looks fairly fit after the knife, doesn't he? But we shall have to cut higher up. The gas again. I'm afraid he'll be dead before to-morrow. Come into the operating-theatre. It's very well equipped."

I refused that invitation. I walked stiffly out of the Butcher's Shop of Corbie past the man who had lost both arms and both legs, that vital trunk, past rows of men lying under blankets, past a stench of mud and blood and anaesthetics, to the fresh air of the gateway, where a column of ambulances had just arrived with a new harvest from the fields of the Somme.

"Come in again, any time!" shouted out the cheery colonel, waving his hand.

I never went again, though I saw many other Butcher's Shops in the years that followed, where there was a great carving of human flesh which was of our boyhood, while the old men directed their sacrifice, and the profiteers grew rich, and the fires of hate were stoked up at patriotic banquets and in editorial chairs.

- CHAPTER 3 -

HOW I FILMED THE SOMME

by Geoffrey Malins

THE FAMOUS FILM of the Battle of the Somme has become one of the most iconic set of images ever created. The footage was shot jointly by Geoffrey H. Malins, who tended to concentrate on the sector north of La Boiselle, and John McDowell whom chiefly filmed the events around Mametz and Fricourt. Malins recorded what had occurred during the making of his film for posterity and published a complete account of his role in filming the infamous battle in his book *How I Filmed The War*.

Their film of the Battle of the Somme has gone on to become one of the most famous documentary films in history. The excellent text provides an invaluable companion to those astonishing images and also gives a unique perspective on the battle from the point of view of a noncombatant who was nonetheless right in the thick of things.

* * * * *

THE TIME FOR WHICH ENGLAND HAS BEEN preparing during these past two awful years is here. We are now on the threshold of tremendous happenings. The Great Offensive is about to begin. What will be the result?

We see the wonderful organisation of our vast armies, and we know the firm and resolute methods of our General Staff - as I have seen and known them during the war - would leave nothing to be desired. As a machine, it is the most wonderful that was ever created.

My position as Official Kinematographer has afforded me unique opportunities to gain knowledge of the whole system required to wage the most terrible war that has ever been known to mankind. I have not let these opportunities slip by.

The great day was coming; there was a mysterious something which affected everyone at G.H.Q. There was no definite news to hand; nobody, with the exception of those directly concerned, knew when and where the blow was to be struck. Some thought on the northern part of our line, others the centre; others, again, the south. In the home, in the streets, in the cafés and gardens, the one topic of conversation was - the coming Great Offensive.

I was told by a colonel that my chance to make history was coming. That was all. But those few words conveyed an enormous lot to me. Later in the day I was told by a captain to proceed to the front line, to choose a suitable position wherein to fix up my camera. Our section facing Gouerment was suggested to me as the place where there was likely to be the most excitement, and I immediately set out for that section. During the journey I was held up by a large body of our men, who turned out afterwards to be the London Scottish. They were formed up in a square, and in the centre was a general, with his staff officers, addressing the men. His words thrilled the hearts of every one who heard them:

"Gentlemen of the London Scottish: Within the next few days you will take part in the greatest battle in the history of the world. To you has been entrusted the taking and holding of Gouerment... England is looking to you to free the world from slavery and militarism that is epitomized in the German nation and German Kultur... Gentlemen, I know you will not fail, and from the bottom of my heart I wish you the best of luck."

I waited until the address was finished, and then proceeded to a certain place, striking out on the left and trudging through innumerable communication trenches, at times up to my knees in mud and water. Eventually I reached an eminence facing the village of Gouerment. It was in a valley. The German trenches ran parallel with my position, and on the right I could discern the long green ribbon of grass termed 'No Man's Land,' stretching as far as the eye could see. The whole front of the German lines was being shelled by our heavy guns; the place was a spitting mass of smoke and flame. Salvo after salvo was being poured from our guns.

"What an inspiring sight," I said to an officer standing by my side, "and these shells were made by the women of England."

"Well," he said, "you see Gommecourt; that's all coming down in a day or two. Every gun, large and small, will concentrate its fire on it, and level it to the ground. That's your picture."

"In that case," I replied, "I shall want to be much nearer our front line. I must get within five hundred yards of it. What a sight! What a film it will be!"

I stood watching the bombardment for some time, then fixing my camera position, I returned. Divisional H.Q. told me I should be informed in ample time when the attack was to be made.

That afternoon I returned to G.H.Q., but the best laid schemes of mice and men aft gang agley. I was told that night to prepare immediately to proceed to the H.Q. of a certain Division, with instructions to attach myself to them for the next week; all particulars would be given to me in the morning.

I received my instructions next morning. I was to proceed to the Division, report myself, and I should receive all the information and assistance I required. With parting wishes for the best of luck, and "don't come back wounded," I left H.Q., and proceeded by car to the Company H.Q., where I was received with every courtesy by General ——.

He told me the best thing to do was to go to Divisional H.Q. and see the General. He had been informed of my arrival, and the final details could be arranged with him, such as the best points of vantage for fixing up my camera. Accordingly I hurried off to Divisional H.Q. and met the General. On being ushered into his room, I found him sitting at a table with a large scale map of a certain section of our line before him. He looked the very incarnation of indomitable will, this General of the incomparable —— Division.

I quickly explained my mission, and told him I should like to go to the front trenches to choose my position.

"Certainly," he said, "that is a very wise plan, but if you will look here I will show you the spot which, in my opinion, will make an ideal place. This is the German position. This, of course, is Beaumont Hamel, which is our objective. This is as far as we are going; it will be a pivot from which the whole front south of us will radiate. We are going to give the village an intense bombardment this afternoon, at 4 o'clock; perhaps you would like to obtain that?"

"Yes, sir," I replied, "it is most necessary to my story. What guns are you using?"

"Everything, from trench mortars to 15-inch howitzers. We are going to literally raze it to the ground. It is one of the strongest German redoubts, and it's not going to be an easy job to occupy it; but we achieved the impossible at Gallipoli, and with God's help we will win here. There is a spot here in our firing trench called 'Jacob's Ladder,'" and pointing to the map, he showed it me.

"That certainly looks a most excellent point, sir," I said. "What is the distance from Bosche lines?"

"About 150 yards. They 'strafe' it considerably, from what I am told; but, of course, you will have to take your chance, the same as all my other officers."

"That is unavoidable, sir. The nature of my work does not permit me to be in very comfortable places, if I am to get the best results."

"Right," he said, "if you will report to Brigade H.Q. the Brigade Major will give you what orderlies you require, and you had better draw rations with them while you are there. He has instructions to give you every assistance."

"Oh, by the way, sir, what time does the mine go up?"

"Ten minutes to zero," he replied. "You quite understand, don't you? Major —— will give you zero time to-morrow night."

After lunching with the General I started off for Brigade H.Q. The weather was vile. It had been raining practically without break for several days, and was doing its best to upset everything and give us as much trouble as possible.

What an enormous number of munition waggons and lorries I passed on the road; miles and miles of them, all making for the front line. "Ye gods!" I thought, "Bosche is certainly going to get it."

I reached my destination about 2.30. What a "strafe" there was going on! The concussion of what I afterwards found out was our 15-inch howitzers was terrible. The very road seemed to shake, and when I opened the door of the temporary Brigade H.Q., one gun which went off close by shook the building to such an extent that I really thought for the moment a shell had struck the house.

"Captain ——, I presume?" said I, addressing an officer seated at a long table making out reports and giving them over to waiting dispatch riders. The room was a hive of industry.

"Gad, sir," he said, "are you the kinema man? I am pleased to see you. Take a seat, and tell me what you want. You are the last person I expected to see out here. But, seriously, are you really going to film 'The Day'?"

"Yes," I replied.

"Where do you propose to take it?"

"General —— suggested 'Jacob's Ladder.'"

"What?" came a startled chorus from about half a dozen other officers. "Take photos from 'Jacob's Ladder,'" they repeated in tones of amazement. "Good Lord! it's an absolute death-trap. Bosche strafes it every day, and it's always covered by snipers."

"Well," I said, "it certainly seems by the map to be an ideal place to get the mine going up and the advance over 'No Man's Land.'"

"Granted, but - well! - it's your shoot. Will you let us introduce the doctor? You'll need him."

"Gentlemen," I said, with mock gravity, "I assure you it would be most difficult for me to receive a more cordial welcome." This remark caused some laughter. Turning to the Captain, I said: "Will you give me an orderly? One who knows the trenches, as I wish to go there this afternoon to film the 'strafe' at 4 o'clock. I shall stay down there for the next few days, to be on the spot for 'The Day,' and ready for anything that follows."

"Certainly," he said. "Have you got a trench map? What about blankets and grub?"

"I have my blanket and some provisions, but if I can draw some bully and biscuits, I shall manage quite well."

Having secured supplies and filled my knapsack, I strapped it on my shoulder, fixed the camera-case on my back and, handing the tripod to another man, started off. I had hardly got more than two hundred yards when the Captain ran up to me and said that he had just had a 'phone message from D.H.Q., saying that the General was going to address the men on the following day, before proceeding to battle. Would I like to film the scene? It would take place about 10 A.M. Naturally, I was delighted at the prospect of such a picture, and agreed to be on the field at the time mentioned. Then with a final adieu we parted.

The weather was still vile. A nasty, drizzly mist hung over everything. The appearance of the whole country was much like it is on a bad November day at home. Everything was clammy and cold. The roads were covered to a depth of several inches with slimy, clayey mud. Loads of munitions were passing up to the Front. On all sides were guns, large and small. The place bristled with them, and they were so cunningly hidden that one might pass within six feet of them without being aware of their existence. But you could not get away from the sounds. The horrible dinning continued, from the sharp rat-tat-tat-tat of the French 75mm., of which we had several batteries in close proximity, and from the bark of the 18-pounders to the crunching roar of the 15-inch howitzer. The air was literally humming with shells. It seemed like a race of shrieking devils, each trying to catch up with the one in front before it reached its objective.

Salvo after salvo; crash after crash; and in the rare moments of stillness, in this nerve-shattering prelude to the Great Push, I could hear the sweet warblings of a lark, as it rose higher and higher in the murky, misty sky.

At one place I had to pass through a narrow lane, and on either side were hidden batteries, sending round upon round into the German trenches, always under keen observation from enemy-spotting balloons and aeroplanes. The recent shell-holes in the roadway made me pause before proceeding further. I noticed a sergeant of the Lancashire Fusiliers at the entrance to a thickly sand-bagged shelter, and asked him if there was another way to the section of the front line I sought.

"No, sir," he said, "that is the only way; but it's mighty unhealthy just now. The Hun is crumpling it with his 5.9-inch H.E., and making a tidy mess of the road. But he don't hit our guns, sir. He just improves their appearance by making a nice little frill of earth around them, he does, and - look out, sir; come in here.

"Here she comes!"

With a murderous shriek and horrible splitting roar a German shell burst on the roadway about fifty yards away.

"That is Fritz's way of making love, sir," he said, with a chuckle; which remark admirably reflects the marvellous morale of our men.

"Have they been shelling the avenues much?" I asked, referring to the various communication trenches leading to the front line.

"Yes, sir. Nos. 1, 2 and 3 are being severely crumped. I would suggest No. 5, sir; it's as clear as any of them. I should advise you to get along this lane as fast as possible. I have been here some time, so I know Fritz's little ways."

He saluted, and like a mole disappeared into his dug-out as I moved away.

I told my man to keep about ten yards behind me, so that in the event of a shell bursting nearby one or the other of us would have a chance of clearing.

"Now," I said, "let it go at a double. Come on," and with head well forward I raced up the road.

Altogether, with my camera, I was carrying about seventy pounds in weight, so you can guess it was no easy matter. There was about another 150 yards to go, when I heard the ominous shriek of a German shell.

"Down in the ditch," I yelled. "Lie flat," and suiting the action to the word, I flung myself down in the mud and water near a fallen tree. Crash came the shell, and it exploded with a deafening roar more on the side of the road than the previous one, and near enough to shower mud and water all over me as I lay there.

"Now then," I yelled to my man, "double-up before they range the next one," and jumping up we raced away. Not before I had got well clear, and near the old railway station, did I stay and rest. While there several shells crashed in and around the road we had just left. I was glad I was safely through.

With the exception of the usual heavy shelling, getting down to the front trench was quite uneventful. My objective was a place called "The White City," so called because it is cut out of the chalk-bank of our position facing Beaumont Hamel. Getting there through the communication trenches was as difficult as in the winter. In places the mud and water reached my knees, and when you had come to the end of your journey you were as much like dirty plaster-cast as anything possibly could be.

After three-quarters of an hour's trudging and splashing I reached "The White City," and turned down a trench called "Tenderloin Street." About one hundred yards on my right, at the junction of "King Street" and "St. Helena Street," my guide pointed me out the Brigade dug-out. Depositing my camera and outfit close to some sandbags I went inside and introduced myself. Four officers were present.

"By Jove!" said one, "you are welcome. Have a drink. Here's a cigarette."

"Here you are," said another, "have a match. Now tell us all the news from home. My word, we haven't heard a blessed thing for days. Have you really come to photograph 'The Day'?"

"Yes," I replied. "But I have come this afternoon to look round, and to film the 'strafe' at Beaumont Hamel. You know the trenches round here: where can I see the village to the best advantage?"

"Well," said one, "there are several places, but Bosche is 'hating' us rather this afternoon, and the firing trench is anything but healthy. He's been properly dosing us with 'whizz-bangs,' but you know he *will* have his bit of fun. You see, when Fritz starts we let off a few 'flying pigs' in return, which undoubtedly disturbs his peace of mind."

"By my map, a spot called 'Lanwick Street' seems likely," I said. "It's bang opposite the village, and they are putting the 15-inch on the eastern corner. If you will be good enough to guide me, I will have a look now; it will take me some time to fix up my camera in reasonable safety."

"You won't find much safety there," he replied. "We have practically to rebuild the parapet every night, but only for a few more days, thank Heaven! Anyway, come along."

We proceeded by way of "King Street" to "Lanwick Street," and several times we had to fall flat in the trench bottom to escape being hit by shells. They seemed at times to burst almost overhead. The "whizz-bangs" which Fritz puts over are rather little beggars; you have no time to dodge them. They come with a "phut" and a bang that for sheer speed knocks spots off a flash of lightning. One only thinks to duck when the beastly thing has gone off.

"Lanwick Street" was the usual sort of trench. At one end was an artillery observation officer, correcting the range of his guns.

"Go easy, won't you?" he said to me. "Bosche has an idea we use this corner for something rather important. If he sees your camera we shall certainly receive his attention. For Heaven's sake, keep your head down."

"Right-o!" I said. "Lend me your periscope; I will have a look at the ground first through that."

I looked on the village, or rather the late site of it. It was absolutely flattened out, with the exception of a few remaining stumps of trees, which used to be a beautiful wood, near which the village nestled.

"That's been done by our guns in five days; some mess, eh?"

"My word, yes. Now about this afternoon's bombardment; they are working on the left-hand corner."

I chose a spot for working and fixing up my tripod, and waited until 4.30 P.M.

In the meantime, with the aid of a stick, I gradually pushed away several sandbags which interfered with my view on the parapet. To do this it was necessary to raise myself head and shoulders above the top and, with one arm pushed forward, I worked the bags clear. I felt much better when that job was done.

"You're lucky," said the A.O. "I had one of my periscopes hit clean by a bullet this morning. Fritz must be having a nap, or he would have had you for a cert."

"Anyway," I replied, "it gives me a comparatively clear view now."

Time was drawing near. I prepared my camera by clothing it in an old piece of sacking, and gently raising it on to the tripod I screwed it tight. Then gradually raising my head to the view-finder, I covered the section which was going to be "strafed," and wrapping my hand in a khaki handkerchief, waited.

Our guns were simply pouring shells on the Bosche. The first of the 15-inch came over and exploded with a deafening roar. The sight was stupefying.

I began to expose my film, swinging the camera first on one side then the other. Shell after shell came roaring over; one dropped on the remaining walls of a château, and when the smoke had cleared there was absolutely nothing left. How in the world anything could live in such a maelstrom of explosive it is difficult to conceive.

I continued to expose my film at intervals until about 6 o'clock, and twice I had to snatch my camera down hastily and take shelter, for the "whizz-bangs" came smashing too close for safety.

I was just taking down my camera when several shells exploded in the trenches about fifteen yards behind us. Then a man came running into our traverse: "Shure, sor," he said, "and it's gas-shells the dirty swine are sending over. My eyes seem to be burning out." His eyes were undoubtedly bad. Tears were pouring down his cheeks, and he was trying to ease the pain by binding his handkerchief over them. Then I smelt the gas, and having had a previous dose at Vernilles, and not wishing for further acquaintance with it, I bade my man rush as quickly as possible back to "The White City."

I got back to H.Q. dug-out just in time for tea. I told the officers present of my success in filming the "strafe," and I learned that it was the first time Fritz had put tear-shells over them. "We must certainly prepare our goggles," they said.

"Have you seen 'Jacob's Ladder'?" enquired one of the officers.

"No," I replied, "I shall wait until dusk. It will then be safer to move about."

We sat smoking and talking about the prospects of the "Big Push," and at last we all lapsed into silence, which was broken by the arrival of a lieutenant. The Captain looked up from his bench. "Hullo, what's up? Any news?"

"Oh, no; nothing much, sir," said he, "but H.Q. wishes me to go out for a raid to-night. They want a Bosche to talk to; there are a few things they want to know. We haven't brought one in for several nights now. They asked me to go out again; I said, if there was one to be had my Company would bring him along."

"Right-o!" said the Captain. "Who are you taking?"

"—— for one, and a few men - the same lot that have been across with me before. H.Q. specially want to know the actual results of the heavy 'strafe.' They are going to cease fire to-night, between twelve and one. I want to find out where their machine guns are fixed up ——" And so the conversation went on.

At that moment another officer came in, and I got him to show me round 'Jacob's Ladder.' We went through "King Street" again, and followed the trench until we arrived at the place. The formation of this point was extraordinary.

A stranger coming upon it for the first time would undoubtedly get a slight shock for, upon turning into a traverse, you come abruptly upon an open space, as if the trench had been sliced off, leaving an opening from which you could look down upon our front line trenches, not only upon them but well in front of them.

I was on the bank of a small valley; leading down from this position were about twenty-five steps, hence the name 'Jacob's Ladder.' Our parapet still followed down, like the handrail of a staircase, only of course much higher.

The position from a photographic point of view was admirable, and I doubt whether on any other part of our front such a suitable point could be found. "Jove!" I said, "this is the ideal place. I will definitely decide upon it."

"If you look carefully over here you will see the Bosche line quite plainly. They are about seventy yards away, and at that point we are going to put a barrage of fire on their second line with our Stokes guns. We are going to do that from 'Sunken Road,' midway in 'No Man's Land.' Can you see it there?"

"Yes," I replied; "splendid. As soon as I have got the mine exploding, and our men going over the parapet and across 'No Man's Land,' I can immediately - if all's well - swing my camera on to the barrage and film that. This is a wonderful position."

"It rests entirely with Fritz now. If he does not crump this place you will be all right, but they are sure to plaster our front trench as soon as they see us go over."

"Well, I must risk that," I said.

And we turned and retraced our steps to the "White City," where I bade my companion good night, and returned to film the scene of the General's speech to his men the following morning.

*   *   *   *   *

Rain, rain, rain. It was like a dull, dismal December night. Owing to the tramping of hundreds of feet up and down the trenches, they became like a quagmire. We slipped and slid, clutching to the sticky, clay walls, and floundering up to our knees in holes, and, to make matters worse, Bosche, who knew that this was the time we brought up fresh munitions, crumped the Fifth Avenue as hard as he could. One or two shells crashed into the trench on the way up, and I had to pass over two working parties (by the aid of a candle-light, screened) searching for, and placing the remains of their comrades in sacks.

Good God! It's a hellish game; and the terror of war gripped one's heartstrings that night. The momentary flash of the exploding shells lighted up the faces of the men with ghastly vividness, some grinding out curses then groping blindly on. I was glad when the journey was ended, and I turned into a dug-out in the village to rest for the night.

Next morning a misty, drizzly pall still hung over everything. I

(Above) Sir Philip Gibbs, one of five official British reporters during the First World War.

(Below) Captain Henry Gilbert Nobbs of the London Rifle Brigade.

(Above) Geoffrey Malins filming the preliminary bombardment of the "Big Push", July 1st 1916.

(Below) Robert Derby Holmes of the 22nd London Battalion, Queen's Royal West Surrey Regiment.

(Above) Isaac Alexander Mack, Captain of the 101ˢᵗ Trench Mortar Battery.

(Above) Soldiers fix bayonets in readiness for an attack on the Somme.

(Below) During the early stages of the battle a communication trench is used for a well-earned rest by a ration party of the Royal Irish Rifles.

(Above) The attack upon German trenches by British troops, 1ˢᵗ July 1916. The figures of the advancing men can be seen against the white of the trenches, excavated from the chalk soil.

(Below) An Allied 9.2-inch gun fires on German positions during the preliminary bombardment.

(Above) In preparation for the assault on Beaumont Hamel, the 1ˢᵗ Lancashire Fusiliers fix their bayonets.

(Below) During afternoon of the first day of the battle, the Seaforth Highlanders assemble for roll call near Beaumont Hamel.

(Above) An allied soldier puts his Lewis light machine gun in to action near Ovillers, July 1916.

(Below) A Vickers machine-gun team operate their weapon wearing the primitive anti-gas helmets of the period, July 1916.

(Above) A Lewis gun captured by the Germans is transported away in triumph, July 1916.

(Below) At a dressing station situated in a church yard, wounded British soldiers are treated and given immediate first aid.

(Above) Captured German soldiers who were wounded in the fighting, are seen through barbed wire at near Morlancourt.

(Below) A shell hole between Montauban and Carnoy is filled with the bodies of dead German soldiers.

(Above) British troops pictured at Mametz Wood, beginning the arduous task of digging trenches.

(Below) Wounded German soldiers are handed water, 30th July 1916.

The 4th Battalion, the Worcester Regiment (29th Division), resting on their way to the trenches, at Acheux. Wire cutters can be seen attached to their rifles.

(Above) Pushing through the wire near Thièpval, men of the Wiltshire Regiment attack, August 1916.

(Below) The shallow dug outs of a front line trench are occupied by the men of the Border Regiment, at rest near Thièpval Wood.

(Above) Near Ginchy, British wounded troops are attended to, despite the enemy shells exploding in the background, 14th September 1916.

(Below) On 15th September 1916, British tanks first went in to action.
Taken in 'Chimpanzee Valley', this picture shows a 'C' Company Mark I tank on that day.

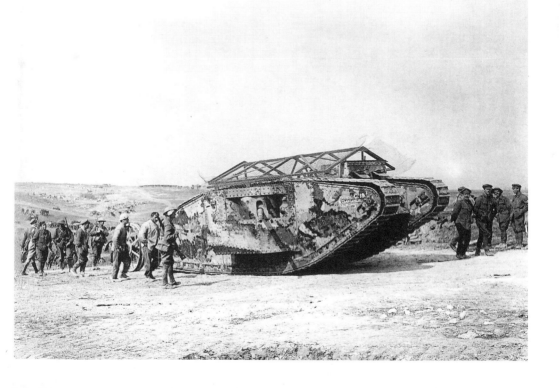

(Above) The destruction caused in Deliville Wood is shown here as ammunition limbers of the 35ᵗʰ Field Battery, The Royal Field Artillery pass through.

(Below) Reserve troops armed with rifles, mortars and Lewis guns await the order to attack near Ginchy.

(Above) A crew operates their 8-inch howitzer in Aveluy Wood, September 1916.

(Below) Empty shell cases are piled high in this dump at Fricourt, September 1916.

(Above) Returning from the front are a wounded Grenadier Guardsman and a German prisoner. Taken near Ginchy, 25th September 1916.

(Below) Then and Now: A soldier of the Border Regiment is imposed on to an image of the trenches as they are today. These works were uncovered by the La Boisselle study group.

(Above) The view from the German front line trenches at La Boiselle looking towards Albert. The spire on the right of the photograph was capped by the famous hanging statue of the Virgin Mary.

(Below) A short service of remembrance is held annually on the lip of the Lochnagar mine crater at 7.20 A.M. on 1ˢᵗ July. The huge scale of the explosion which was unleashed can still be clearly seen.

(Above) The British cemetery near Ovillers is one of dozens which mark the landscape of the Somme region. The scale of the sacrifice is clearly conveyed by the size of this site.

(Below) The heroic deeds of the 36ᵗʰ 'Ulster' Division are commemorated today by this gracious monument. Every year on 1ˢᵗ July a service of commemoration is held on this spot.

wondered how in the world our men were going to attack under such conditions, and to-morrow was "The Day." I pitied them with all my heart and soul. And then I thought of myself, and my own particular job. I couldn't possibly "take" in such disgusting weather. The result would be an absolute failure. I controlled my feelings, and hoped for the best.

The time arrived for the General's speech. Reaching the field, I found all the men mustered up. The General had just arrived. I started to film the scenes as they presented themselves to me. Jove! The speech was the most impressive that I had ever heard. I will give it as it was spoken, as near as I can. I do not think that it has been published before:

"*Officers and men of the West Riding Field Company, R.E., and - Battalion, Royal Fusiliers:*

"*I hoped yesterday to be able to come and wish you good luck, on the first anniversary of the engagement in Gully Ravine, there the Royal Fusiliers took the Turkish fifth line of trenches. Owing to the rain, however, and to the discomfort to which you would have been placed, I postponed my visit until to-day.*

"*I want to tell you something of the situation as it now stands. You are probably aware that we are now taking part in the greatest battle ever fought by British troops. Not only is it of far more importance than any fight since Waterloo, but the numbers engaged far exceed any assembly of troops in former days. The strength of this army, - the Fourth Army - under General Sir H. S. Rawlinson, is - times as large as the force of British troops at Mons, when we first came out a year and a half ago.*

"*The importance of winning a great victory is so great that nothing has been left undone to ensure success. But the higher Commanders know - and I know - that all the best arrangements in the world cannot win battles. Battles are won by infantry, and it is to the battalions like yourself that we look to gain a great victory, equal to the great victory which the Russians have obtained this month.*

"*The Germans are shut in all round. On their northern flank they are shut in by the British Navy, on the eastern flank pressed back by the Russians, on the southern flank the Italians are advancing, and this week,* on the western flank, certain Divisions of the French and many Divisions of the British are determined to break their line and drive them back to their own country.

"Officers and men of the - Battalion, the Royal Fusiliers: You are very fortunate in having this opportunity to add to the high honours already gained by your distinguished regiment. Not only, however, are you fighting for your battalion and your regiment, you are fighting to maintain against the Germans the same high reputation which you have won for the - Division on the Gallipoli Peninsula. More than that, you are fighting for your country, and also you are fighting for Christianity and Humanity. You are fighting for truth and justice against oppression. We are fighting for our liberty against slavery.

"It is now thirty-three years since I was first associated with the Royal Fusiliers, the regiment I have looked up to during all my service as a pattern of smartness and efficiency. I have served with you in Gibraltar, Egypt, and many stations in India; also at Aldershot, and on the Gallipoli Peninsula during the past year. There is no regiment in the service in which I have had a higher confidence, and I hope next week to be able to assemble you again and to congratulate you on the great victory that you are going to win for me, as commanding this Division, and for your country."

The faces of the men shone with a new light. It seemed as if they had seen a sight which other mortals were not allowed to look upon. As upright as poplars, chests well forward and heads thrown back, their souls seemed to speak out of their inflexible determination to win. They marched away, going to that stretch of land from which many have never returned - giving their lives for freedom and the honour of England.

I turned and gave a parting wave of the hand to a group of officers standing by.

"See you to-night," I said, "at the 'White City.' We will drink to the health of 'The Day,'" and with a parting laugh I moved a way.

I found out through H.Q. that some of our 15-inch howitzers were in the vicinity, so I decided to film them without delay, to work them into the story of the battle. I discovered their position on my map. I reached the battery. The state of the ground was indescribable. It was more like a "sea of mud," and standing in the middle of this morass was the giant gun, for all the world like a horrible frog squatting on its haunches. Each time it breathed it belched out flame and smoke with the most unearthly crash that could possibly be produced, and with each breath there flew with it a mass of metal and high explosive weighing fourteen hundred pounds, scattering death and destruction for hundreds of yards round the point of impact in the German defences, so that our boys might find it easier to force their way through.

I filmed the firing several times, from various points of view, and when standing only about fifteen yards away the concussion shook the ground like a miniature earthquake. On one occasion, indeed, it lifted my camera and tripod in the air, driving it crashing into my chest. I had unknowingly placed myself in the danger zone which forms a semi-circle on either side of the muzzle when fired, the force being at times so great as to tear trees up by the roots and send them crashing to the ground.

The prospects for "The Day" were certainly bad. As one burly Lancashire lad said to me: "the Devil was looking after his own; but we are going to beat them, sir." That was the spirit of all the men I met there.

I went direct to B.H.Q. to get a full supply of film stock before going to the front line. I wished to get there early, to have a final look round and a discussion with the officers.

A man I knew was there, looking for all the world like a man down and out. He had a face as long as a fiddle, and several other officers were looking just as glum. "You're a cheerful lot," I said. "What's up? Anything wrong?"

"Yes, rather," they replied, "the —— day is postponed for forty-eight hours."

"Great Scott! Why?" I asked.

"The weather," he answered laconically. "It's quite impossible for our chaps to go over the top in such sticky stuff. They wouldn't stand an earthly. As I said before, it's doing its best to upset the whole affair. I know the men will be awfully disappointed. We can hardly hold them back now - but there, I suppose the Commander-in-Chief knows best. Undoubtedly it's a wise decision. The weather may break - God knows it couldn't be worse!"

At that moment the Brigade-General came in. He was looking quite bright.

"I hear 'The Day' has been postponed, sir," I said. "Is that official?"

"Yes," he said. "If the weather improves ever such a little it will pay us for waiting, and of course it will suit you much better?"

"Rather," I replied. "It also gives me more time to film the preliminary scenes. I shall, however, keep to my programme, and go to the trenches this afternoon."

I packed all my apparatus together, put some bully and biscuits in my bag, and started off once more for the trenches. I admit that on the journey thoughts crept into my mind, and I wondered whether I should return. Outwardly I was merry and bright, but inwardly - well, I admit I felt a bit nervous. And yet, I had an instinctive feeling that all would be well, that I need not worry. Such is the complex mystery of the human mind, battling within itself against its own knowledge, its own decisions, its own instincts. And yet there is a predominating force which seems to shuffle itself out of the midst of that chaotic state of mind, and holds itself up as a beacon-light, saying "Follow me, believe in me, let me guide you, all will be well." And it is the man who allows himself to be guided by that mysterious something, which for the want of a better name we may call "instinct," who benefits, both spiritually and materially, by it.

The usual big gun duel was proceeding with its usual intensity, but we were putting over about fifty shells to the Huns' one. "Crump" fell both ahead and behind me, compelling me, as before, to fall flat upon the ground. I reached the "Fifth Avenue." The trench was full of men taking down munitions. The news of the postponement had by some means reached them; they also were looking rather glum.

Ye Gods, I thought, it's very nearly worth while to risk walking along the top. In places there was quite two feet of mud and water to wallow through.

"Fritz is crumping down the bottom of the Avenue, sir," said a Tommy to me; "just caught several of our lads - dirty blighters: right in the trench, sir."

"Thanks," I replied.

Thinking there might be an opportunity of getting some scenes of shell-bursts, I hurried on as fast as conditions would permit. With men coming up, and myself and others going down, with full packs on, it was most difficult to squeeze past each other. At times it was impossible, so climbing up on to the parapet, I crawled into another traverse further along.

Just then another shell burst lower down, but well away from the trench, hurting no one. I eventually reached the "White City" without mishap, and was greeted enthusiastically by the officers present.

"What's the programme now?"

"I am waiting for the final kick-off," I said. "Are you going to give me a good show? And don't forget," I said, "hold back some of your bayonet-work on Fritz until I get there with my machine."

"But you're not coming after us with that affair, are you?"

"Yes, certainly; bet your life I shan't be far behind. As soon as you get into Bosche trenches I shall be there; so don't forget - get there."

From the corner some one shouted: "Tell brother Fritz if he gets out of 'the limits,' won't you?" This remark caused much laughter.

"Where have you heard that term used?" I enquired. "'Limits' is a technical term."

"Yes, I heard it used once, a year or two ago. I was staying at a small place called Steyning, near Brighton. A Film Company was taking scenes in the village and on the downs. They had about two hundred horsemen and an immense crowd, and were rehearsing a scene for what I was told was a representation of the Battle of Worcester. It was some fight. The camera man was continually shouting out to them to keep in 'the limits' (I assumed he meant the angle of view). As I say, it was some fight. Everything went well until a section of the men, who were supposed to run away, got a few genuine knocks on the head and, wishing to get their own back, they continued fighting. It was the funniest thing in the world. Of course the camera was stopped, and the scene retaken."

"That's extraordinary," I replied. "Do you know that I was the chap who filmed that scene? It was for a film play called 'King Charles.' It's very peculiar how one meets. I remember that incident quite well."

I again filmed various scenes of the Germans "strafing" our lines. Our guns, as usual, were crashing out. They were pouring concentrated fire on the Hawthorn Redoubt, a stronghold of the Germans, and thinking it would yield an excellent picture, I made my way to a point of vantage, whence I could get an unobstructed field of view. There was only one place, and that was a point directly opposite. To get there it was necessary to cross a sunken road about twenty-five feet wide. But it was under continual fire from German machine guns, and being broad daylight it was absolutely asking for trouble, thick and unadulterated, to attempt to cross it. I was advised not to do so, and I admit I ought to have taken the advice. Anyway, the opportunity of getting such a fine scene of a barrage of fire was too strong, and for once my cautionary instincts were at fault.

To reach the sunken road was comparatively easy. You had only to walk along our front line trench, and fall down flat on the ground when a German shell burst near you, then proceed. I reached the junction where the road ran across at right angles, and from the shelter of our parapet the road looked the quietest place on earth. It appeared easy enough to me to jump up quickly, run across and drop on the further side in our trench.

"Ridiculously easy! I'm going across," I said to my man. "When I'm over I'll throw a cord across for you to tie my tripod on to; then I'll pull it across. It will save you attempting it."

I tied the camera on my shoulders, so as to have my arms quite free. I was now ready. The firing was renewed with redoubled vigour. Shells I could see were falling on the Hun lines like hailstones. "Jove!" I said to myself, "I shall miss it. Here goes."

Clambering up to the road level, I sprawled out flat and lay perfectly still for a few seconds, with my heart jumping like a steam engine.

Nothing happened. I gradually drew up my leg, dug the toe of my boot in the ground, and pushed myself forward bit by bit. So far, so good: I was half-way across. I was congratulating myself on my easy task. "What in the world am I lying here for?" I asked myself; "why shouldn't I run the remaining distance?" And suiting the action to the word, I got up - and found trouble! I had barely raised myself to my hands and knees when, with a rattle and a rush, a stream of bullets came swishing by, some striking the ground on my left, about nine feet away.

I took the whole situation in in a flash. To lie there was almost certain death; to stand up was worse; to go back was as bad as going forward. What happened afterwards I don't know. I could hear the bullets whizzing by my head with an ugly hiss. The next moment, with a jump and a spring, I landed head first in the trench on the opposite side. For the moment I did not know whether I was hit or not. I unstrapped my camera, to see if it had caught any bullets, but, thank Heaven, they had cleared it. Some of our men were standing looking aghast at me, and wondering what the devil it was that had made such a sudden dive into their midst. The look on their faces was just too funny for words; I had to roar with laughter, and, realising that I was safe, they also joined in.

But I was not out of the wood yet, for brother Fritz immediately turned "whizz-bangs" on to us. "Phut-bang," "phut-bang," they came. Every one scampered for cover. Needless to say, I did so too. Five minutes went by. All the time these souvenirs dropped around us, but luckily none of them got any direct hits on our trench.

I thought I would wait another five minutes, to see if Bosche would cease fire. But not he. He was rather cross about my crossing the road safely.

Time went by. Still the firing continued. I decided to risk throwing the cord and pulling over my tripod. Keeping low, I yelled to my man: he, like a sage, had also taken cover, but hearing my shouts came out.

"The rope is coming," I yelled. "Tug it as a signal, when you have it."

"Right," came the reply.

Three times I threw it before I received the welcome tug at the other end. Then a voice shouted: "Pull away, sir."

I pulled. I had to do it gently, otherwise the broken nature of the ground might damage the head. At last it was safely over, but Bosche had seen something moving across; then he turned his typewriter on again. More bullets flew by, but with the exception of one which struck the metal revolving top and sliced out a piece as evenly as if it had been done by machine, no harm was caused.

I bade one of the men shoulder my tripod. We rushed up the trench as fast as possible, and I thanked Heaven for my escape. When I reached the section where I judged it best to fit up my camera, I gently peeped over the parapet. What a sight. Never in my life had I seen such a hurricane of fire. It was inconceivable that any living thing could exist anywhere near it. The shells were coming over so fast and furious that it seemed as if they must be touching each other on their journey through the air.

To get my camera up was the work of a few seconds. I had no time to put any covering material over it. The risk had to be run, the picture was worth it. Up went my camera well above the parapet and, quickly sighting my object, I started to expose. Swinging the machine first one way then the other, I turned the handle continuously. Pieces of shell were flying and ripping past close overhead. They seemed to get nearer every time. Whether they were splinters from the bursting shells or bullets from machine guns I could not tell, but it got so hot at last that I judged it wise to take cover. I had exposed sufficient film for my purpose, so quickly unscrewing the camera, my man taking the tripod, I hurried into a dug-out for cover. "Jove!" I thought, mopping the perspiration from my head, "quite near enough to be healthy!"

Although the men were all taking cover, they were as happy as crickets over this "strafe." There is nothing a Tommy likes more than to see our artillery plastering Bosche trenches into "Potsdam."

"Well, what's the next move?" I was asked.

"Trench Mortars," I said. "Both 'Flying Pigs' and 'Plum Puddings' ought to make topping scenes."

"Yes," the Captain said. "They are in action this afternoon, and I am in charge of H.T.M. I'll give you a good show. I have only one pit available, as Fritz dropped a 'crump' in the other yesterday, and blew the whole show to smithereens. My sergeant was sitting smoking at the time, and when she blew up it lifted him clean out of the trench, without even so much as scratching him. He turned round to me, and cursed Bosche for spoiling his smoke. He's promised to get his own back on 'Brother Fritz.' Bet your life he will too."

He had hardly ceased speaking, when our dug-out shook as if a mine had gone up close by. I tumbled out, followed by the others. Lumps of earth fell on our heads; I certainly thought the roof was coming in on us. Getting into the trench, the bombardment was still going strong, and looking on my left I saw a dense cloud of smoke in our own firing trench.

"What in the world's up?" I enquired of a man close by.

"Dunno, sir," he said. "I believe it's a Bosche mine. It made enough fuss to be one, yet it seems in such an extraordinary position."

"How about getting round to have a look at it?" I said to ———.

"Right-o," he said; "but you know we can't cross the road there. I think if we back well down, about one hundred yards, we may nip across into No. 2 Avenue. That'll bring us out near 'Jacob's Ladder.'"

"Lead on," I said. "I wish I had known. I came in across the road there," pointing down our firing trench.

"You've got more pluck than I have," he said. "You can congratulate yourself that you are alive. Anyway, come on."

Eventually I reached 'Jacob's Ladder,' and asked an officer what had happened.

"I don't know," he said; "but whatever it was, it's smashed our front trench for about eighty yards: it's absolutely impassable."

Another officer came running up at that moment. "I say," he said, "there's a scene up there for you. A trench mortar gun had a premature burst, and exploded all the munition in the pit; blew the whole lot - men and all - to pieces. It's made a crater thirty yards across. It's a beastly wreck. Can't use that section of the front line. And to make matters worse, Fritz is pumping over tear-shells. Everybody is tickled to death with the fumes."

"Don't cheer me up, will you?" I remarked. "I'm going to film the trench mortar this afternoon, both the H.T.M. and the 2-inch Gee. I can thank my lucky stars I didn't decide to do them earlier. Anyway, here goes; the light is getting rather poor."

The officer with whom I was talking kindly offered to guide me to the spot. Crumps were still falling, and so was the rain. "We'll go through 'Lanwick Street,' then bear to the left, and don't forget to keep your head down."

There are two things I detest more than anything else in the trenches: they are "whizz-bangs" and rats. The latter got mixed up in my feet as I was walking through the trench, and one, more impudent than the rest, when I crouched down to avoid a burst, jumped on to my back and sprang away into the mud.

"We will turn back and go by way of 'White City,' then up King Street. It may be cooler there." It certainly was not healthy in this neighbourhood.

Turning back, I bade my man follow close behind. Entering the main trench, I hurried along, and was quite near the King Street turning when a Hun "crump" came tearing overhead. I yelled out to my man to take cover, and crushed into the entrance of a dug-out myself. In doing so, I upset a canteen of tea over a bucket-fire which one of our lads was preparing to drink. His remarks were drowned in the explosion of the shell, which landed barely twenty-five feet away.

"Now then," I called to my man, "run for it into King Street," and I got there just in time to crouch down and escape another "crump" which came hurtling over. In a flash I knew it was coming very near: I crouched lower. It burst with a sickening sound. It seemed just overhead. Dirt and rubble poured over me as I lay there. I rushed to the corner to see where it had struck. It had landed only twelve feet from the dug-out entrance which I had left only a few seconds before, and it had killed the two men whom I had crushed against, and for the loss of whose tea I was responsible.

It was not the time or place to hang about, so I hurried to the trench-mortar pit to finish my scenes whilst daylight lasted.

I met the officer in charge of the T.M.

"Keep your head down," he shouted, as I turned round a traverse. "Our parapet has been practically wiped out, and there is a sniper in the far corner of the village. He has been dropping his pellets into my show all day, and Fritz has been splashing me with his 'Minnies' to try and find my gun, but he will never get it. Just look at the mess around."

I was looking. It would have beaten the finest Indian scout to try and distinguish the trench from the débris and honeycomb of shell-holes.

"Where the deuce is your outfit?" I said, looking round.

"You follow me, but don't show an inch of head above. Look out." Phut-bang came a pip-squeak. It struck and burst about five yards in front of us. "Brother Fritz is confoundedly inconsiderate," he said. "He seems to want all the earth to himself. Come on; we'll get there this time, and run for it."

After clambering, crawling, running and jumping, we reached a hole in the ground, into which the head and shoulders of a man were just disappearing.

"This is my abode of love," said my guide. "How do you like it?"

I looked down, and at the depth of about twelve feet was a trench mortar. The hole itself was, of course, boarded round with timber, and was about seven feet square. There was a gallery leading back under our parapet for the distance of about eighty feet, and in this were stored the bombs. The men also sheltered there.

I let myself down with my camera and threaded by the numerous "plum puddings" lying there: I fixed my camera up and awaited the order for the men to commence firing.

"Are you ready?" came a voice from above.

"Right, sir," replied the sergeant. I began exposing my film.

"Fire!" the T.M. officer shouted down.

Fire they did, and the concussion nearly knocked me head over heels. I was quite unprepared for such a backblast. Before they fired again, I got a man to hold down the front leg of my tripod. The gun was recharged; the order to fire was given, the lanyard was pulled, but no explosion.

"Hullo, another ——"

"Misfire," was the polite remark of the sergeant. "Those fuses are giving us more trouble than enough."

Another detonator was put on, everything was ready again. Another tug was given. Again no explosion.

Remembering the happenings of the morning in another pit, when a premature burst occurred, I felt anything but comfortable. Sitting in the middle of about one hundred trench mortar bombs, visions of the whole show going up came to me.

Another detonator was put in. "Fire," came the order. Again it failed.

"Look here, sergeant," I said, "if that bally thing happens again I'm off."

"The blessed thing has never been so bad before, sir. Let's have one more try."

Still another detonator was put in. I began turning the handle of my camera. This time it was successful.

"That's all I want," I said. "I'm off. Hand me up my camera. And with due respect to your gun," I said to the T.M. officer, "you might cease fire until I am about fifty yards away. I don't mind risking Brother Fritz's 'strafe,' but I do object to the possibility of being scattered to the four winds of heaven by our own shells." And with a laugh and good wishes, I left him.

"I say," he called out, "come into my dug-out to-night, will you? It's just in front of Fifth Avenue. I shall be there in about half an hour; I have got to give Fritz a few more souvenirs to go on with. There is a little more wire left over there, and the C.O. wants it all 'strafed' away. Do come, won't you? So long. See you later. Keep your head down."

"Right-o!" I said, with a laugh. "Physician, heal thyself. A little higher, and you might as well be sitting on the parapet." He turned round sharply, then dropped on his knees.

"Strafe that bally parapet. I forgot all about it. Fire!" he yelled, and I laughed at the pleasure he was getting out of blowing up Fritz.

I scrambled and slithered back into the recognised trench again, and on my way back filmed the H.T.M., or "Flying Pig," in action. By this time it was getting rather dull, so going to a dug-out, I dropped my apparatus, and had another final look at the position from which I was going to film the great attack in the morning.

*   *   *   *   *

Darkness came, and with it a host of star-shells, or Verey lights, which were shot up high in the air from both the German and our own trenches. They looked for all the world like a huge firework display at the Crystal Palace.

Rain had ceased. The heavens were studded with countless millions of stars. "Great prospects for to-morrow," said one. "I hope it's fine, for the sake of the boys. They are as keen as mustard to go over the top."

As we talked, batch after batch of men came gliding by in their full kit, smoking and chatting. While I was standing there hundreds must have passed me in that narrow trench, quietly going to their allotted positions. Now and again sharp orders were given by their officers.

"How's your section, sergeant? Are you fitted up?"

"Yes, sir," came a voice from the blackness.

"Now, lads, come along: get through as quickly as possible. Post your sentries at once, and be sharp."

It was not long before little red fires were gleaming out of the dug-out entrances, and crowds of men were crouching round, heating their canteens of water, some frying pieces of meat, others heating soup, and all the time laughing and carrying on a most animated conversation. From other groups came the subdued humming of favourite songs. Some were cursing and swearing, but with such a bluntness that, if I may say so, it seemed to take all the profanity from the words.

And these men knew they were going "over the top" in the morning. The day which they had dreamed of was about to materialise. They knew that many would not be alive to-morrow night, yet I never saw a sad face nor heard a word of complaint. My feeling whilst watching these men in the glow of the firelight was almost indescribable. I was filled with awe at their behaviour. I reverenced them more than I had ever done before; and I felt like going down on my knees and thanking God I was an Englishman. No words of mine can fitly describe this wonderful scene. And all the time more men, and still more men, were pouring into the trenches, and munitions of all descriptions were being served out.

The bursting German shells, and the shrieks overhead of the missiles from our own guns, were for the moment forgotten in the immensity of the sights around me. I turned and groped the way back to my shelter and, as I did so, our fire increased in intensity. This was the prelude to the greatest attack ever made in the history of the world, and ere the sun set on the morrow many of these heroes - the Lancashire Fusiliers, Royal Fusiliers, Middlesex, etc. - would be lying dead on the field of battle, their lives sacrificed that civilisation might live.

At last I found a friend, and sitting down to our box-table we had a meal together. Afterwards I wandered out, and entered several other dug-outs, where friends were resting. They all seemed anxious for the morning to come. I met the mining officer.

"I say; let me check my watch by yours," I said. "As the mine is going up at 7.20 I shall want to start my machine about half a minute beforehand."

"Right-o!" he said. We then checked watches. I bade him good night, and also the others, and the best of luck.

"Same to you," they cried in general chorus. "I hope to heavens you get through with it, and show them all at home in England how the boys fight. They will then realise what war really means. Good night, old man."

"Good night," I replied, and then found my way back to the shelter. I rolled myself in a blanket, and tried to sleep.

The night was very cold. I lay shivering in my blanket and could not get warm. The guns were continually crashing out. Shells were bursting just outside with appalling regularity. Suddenly they seemed to quieten down, as if by some means the Germans had got to know of our great plans and were preparing for the blow. Presently everything was comparatively quiet, except for the scurrying of countless rats, running and jumping over my body, as if it was the most natural thing in the world. I expect I must have dozed off to sleep, for when I awoke day was breaking, and the din of the gun-fire was terrific. Innumerable worlds seemed to be crashing together, and it sounded as if thousands of peals of thunder had concentrated themselves into one soul-terrifying roar.

An officer looked in at the entrance at that moment.

"Hullo!" he said. "Are you the 'movie-man'?"

"Yes," I said, sitting up. "What's up?"

"Well, I'm hanged; I'm glad I've found you. Do you know, I asked several Johnnies down the line if you were in the trenches and they laughed at me; asked me if I had been drinking; they thought I was pulling their leg. 'A movie man in the trenches,' they said, in tones of amazement; 'not likely!' I told them that you were here last night, and that you are here to film the attack. Well, anyway, this is what I have come for. The Colonel sent me - you know him - to see if you would film a company of our men in occupation of Sunken Road. They occupied it during the night without a single casualty, by tunnelling for about fifty yards through the parapet, under 'No Man's Land'; then sapped up and into the road. It's a fine piece of work," he said, "and would make a good picture."

"Rather," I said; "I'll come. It will be splendid from the historical point of view. Can you let me have a guide, to show me the quickest and best way?"

"Yes, I will send one of our pioneers; he will guide you," he said. "Let me know how you get on, won't you? And, if possible, when you return call in and see the Colonel. He will be frightfully bucked."

"Right-o!" I said. "By Gad! it's bally cold. My teeth won't hold still. Push that man along, and I'll get off."

"Au revoir," he called out as he left. "See you later."

The guide turned up a few minutes afterwards; he took the tripod, I the camera. I started off and entered King Street, making my way towards the firing trench. I have described in previous chapters what it was like to be under an intense bombardment. I have attempted to analyse my feelings when lying in the trenches with shells bursting directly overhead. I have been in all sorts of places, under heavy shell-fire, but for intensity and nearness - nothing - absolutely nothing - compared with the frightful and demoralising nature of the shell-fire which I experienced during that journey.

I had only just reached King Street, when it started on that section. Bosche was fairly plastering the whole trench, and smashing down our parapets in the most methodical manner. Four men passed me, with horrible wounds; another was being carried on the shoulders of his comrades, one arm being blown clean off, leaving flesh and remnants of cloth hanging down in a horrible manner. The shells fell in front, overhead and behind us.

I bent low and rushed through traverse after traverse, halting when a shell burst in the trench itself round the next bend, sending a ghastly blast of flame and choking fumes full in my face. At one point I halted, hardly knowing which way to go; my guide was crouching as low as possible on the ground. The further I went, the worse it got; shrieking, splitting shells seemed to envelop us. I looked back. The same. In front, another burst; the flames swept right into my face. If I had been standing up it would have killed me without a doubt. To go back was as dangerous as to advance, and to stay where I was - well, it was worse, if anything. Truth to tell, I had gone so far now that I did not like turning back; the picture of our men in Sunken Road attracted me like a magnet.

"Go on," I shouted to the guide. "We'll get through somehow. Are you game?"

"Yes, sir," said he.

We ran round the next traverse, and had to scramble over a heap of débris caused by a shell a few moments before.

"Look out, sir! There are some dead men here, and the parapet has practically disappeared. Get down on your stomach and crawl along."

Phut-bang! The shells crashed on the parapet with the rapidity of machine-gun fire.

I went down, and crawled along over the dead bodies of some of our lads killed only a few minutes before. It couldn't be helped. Purgatory, in all its hideous shapes and forms, could not possibly be worse than this journey. It seemed years getting through that hellish fire.

"How much more?" I yelled out.

"We are quite near now, sir; about twenty yards."

"Rush for it, then - rush."

I did, and my guide pulled up quickly at the entrance of what seemed like a mine.

"Incline in here, sir," he said, and disappeared. I followed. Never in all my experience had I welcomed cover as I did at that moment.

"Hold on a bit," I said, "for five minutes' breathing space."

The tunnel was no more than two feet six inches wide and five feet high. Men inside were passing ammunition from one to the other in an endless chain and disappearing into the bowels of the earth.

The shaft took a downward trend. It was only by squeezing past the munition bearers that we were able to proceed at all, and in some places it was impossible for more than one to crush through at a time. By the light of an electric torch, stuck in the mud, I was able to see the men. They were wet with perspiration, steaming, in fact; stripped to the waist; working like Trojans, each doing the work of six men.

The journey seemed endless. I could tell by the position that I was climbing. My guide was still in front, and letting me know of his whereabouts by shouting: "Straight ahead, sir! Mind this hole!"

The latter part of the shaft seemed practically upright. I dragged my camera along by the strap attached to the case. It was impossible to carry it.

We were nearing daylight. I could see a gleam only a few feet away. At last we came to the exit. My guide was there.

"Keep down low, sir. This sap is only four feet deep. It's been done during the night, about fifty yards of it. We are in 'No Man's Land' now, and if the Germans had any idea we were here, the place would soon be an inferno."

"Go ahead," I said. It was difficult to imagine we were midway between the Hun lines and our own. It was practically inconceivable.

The shell-fire seemed just as bad as ever behind in the trenches, but here it was simply heavenly. The only thing one had to do was to keep as low as possible and wriggle along. The ground sloped downwards. The end of the sap came in sight. My guide was crouching there, and in front of him, about thirty feet away, running at right angles on both sides, was a roadway, overgrown with grass and pitted with shell-holes. The bank immediately in front was lined with the stumps of trees and a rough hedge, and there lined up, crouching as close to the bank as possible, were some of our men. They were the Lancashire Fusiliers, with bayonets fixed, and ready to spring forward.

"Keep low as you run across the road, sir. The Bosche can see right along it; make straight for the other side." With that he ran across, and I followed. Then I set my camera up and filmed the scene. I had to take every precaution in getting my machine in position, keeping it close to the bank, as a false step would have exposed the position to the Bosche, who would have immediately turned on H.E. shrapnel, and might have enfiladed the whole road from either flank.

I filmed the waiting Fusiliers. Some of them looked happy and gay, others sat with stern, set faces, realising the great task in front of them.

I had finished taking my scenes, and asked an officer if the Colonel was there.

"No, but you may find him in 'White City.' He was there about an hour ago. Great heavens," he said, "who would have believed that a 'movie-man' would be here, the nearest point to Bosche lines on the whole front. You must like your job. Hanged if I envy you. Anyway, hope to see you after the show, if I haven't 'gone West.' Cheero," and with that he left me.

Packing up my camera, I prepared to return. Time was getting on. It was now 6.30 a.m. The attack was timed for 7.20. As I wanted to obtain some scenes of our men taking up their final positions, I told my guide to start.

"Duck as low as possible," I said, "when you cross the road."

"We can't go yet, sir; munitions are being brought through, and, as you know, there isn't room to pass one another."

I waited until the last man had come in from the sap, then, practically on hands and knees, made for the sap mouth.

"Cheer up, boys," I shouted to the men as I parted from them, "best of luck; hope to see you in the village."

"Hope so, sir," came a general chorus in reply.

Again I struggled through the narrow slit, then down the shaft and finally into the tunnel. We groped our way along as best we could. The place was full of men. It was only possible to get my tripod and camera along by passing it from one to another. Then as the men stooped low I stepped over them, eventually reaching the other end - and daylight.

The "strafe" was still on, but not quite so violent. Our parapets were in a sorry condition, battered out of all shape.

Returning through King Street, I was just in time to film some of the men fixing bayonets before being sent to their respective stations in the firing trench. The great moment was drawing near. I admit I was feeling a wee bit nervous. The mental and nervous excitement under such conditions was very great. Every one was in a state of suppressed excitement. On the way I passed an officer I knew.

"Are you going over?" I said.

"Rather," he replied, "the whole lot of us. Some stunt, eh!"

"Don't forget," I said, "the camera will be on you; good luck!"

Bidding my man collect the tripod and camera, I made for the position on 'Jacob's Ladder.' But I was to receive a rude shock. The shelling of the morning had practically blown it all down. But there was sufficient for a clearance all around for my purpose, and sufficient shelter against stray bits of shrapnel. I prepared to put up my camera. Not quite satisfied, I left it about thirty yards away, to view the situation quickly, as there were only twenty minutes to go. Hardly had I left the machine than a "whizz-bang" fell and struck the parapet immediately above the ladder, tumbling the whole lot of sandbags down like a pack of cards.

It was a lucky escape for me. The position was absolutely no use now, and I had to choose another. Time was short. I hastily fixed my camera on the side of the small bank, this side of our firing trench, with my lens pointing towards the Hawthorn Redoubt, where the mine - the largest "blown" on the British Front - was going up. It was loaded with twenty tons of a new explosive of tremendous destructive power, and it had taken seven months to build.

Gee, what an awakening for Bosche!

My camera was now set ready to start exposing. I looked along the trench. The men were ready and waiting the great moment.

One little group was discussing the prospects of a race across 'No Man's Land.'

"Bet you, Jim, I'll get there first."

"Right-o! How much?"

"A day's pay," was the reply.

"Take me on, too, will you?" said another hero.

"Yes. Same terms, eh? Good enough."

"Say Bill," he called to his pal, "pay up from my cash if I 'go West.'"

"Shut up, fathead; we have to kill Huns, 'strafe' them."

I turned away to speak to an officer as to the prospects.

"Very good," he said. "I hope they don't plaster our trenches before all the men get out. They are as keen as mustard. Never known them so bright. Look at them now; all smoking."

Our guns were still pounding heavily, and the din and concussion was awful. To hear oneself speak it was absolutely necessary to shout.

"You are in a pretty rocky position," some one said to me. "Fritz will be sure to plaster this front pretty well as soon as our men 'get over.'"

"Can't help it," I said; "my machine must have a clear view. I must take the risk. How's the time going?"

"It's 'seven-ten' now," he said.

"I am going to stand by. Cheero; best of luck!"

I left him, and stood by my machine. The minutes dragged on. Still the guns crashed out. The German fire had died down a bit during the last half-hour. I glanced down our trenches. The officers were giving final instructions. Every man was in his place. The first to go over would be the engineers, to wire the crater. They were all ready, crouching down, with their implements in their hands.

Time: 7.15 A.M.!

Heavens! how the minutes dragged. It seemed like a lifetime waiting there. My nerves were strung up to a high pitch; my heart was thumping like a steam-hammer. I gave a quick glance at an officer close by. He was mopping the perspiration from his brow, and clutching his stick, first in one hand then in the other - quite unconsciously, I am sure. He looked at his watch. Another three minutes went by.

Would nothing ever happen?

* * * * *

Time: 7.19 A.M. My hand grasped the handle of the camera. I set my teeth. My whole mind was concentrated upon my work. Another thirty seconds passed. I started turning the handle, two revolutions per second, no more, no less. I noticed how regular I was turning. (My object in exposing half a minute beforehand was to get the mine from the moment it broke ground.) I fixed my eyes on the Redoubt. Any second now. Surely it was time. It seemed to me as if I had been turning for hours. Great heavens! Surely it had not misfired.

Why doesn't it go up?

I looked at my exposure dial. I had used over a thousand feet. The horrible thought flashed through my mind, that my film might run out before the mine blew. Would it go up before I had time to reload? The thought brought beads of perspiration to my forehead. The agony was awful; indescribable. My hand began to shake. Another 250 feet exposed. I had to keep on.

Then it happened.

The ground where I stood gave a mighty convulsion. It rocked and swayed. I gripped hold of my tripod to steady myself. Then, for all the world like a gigantic sponge, the earth rose in the air to the height of hundreds of feet. Higher and higher it rose, and with a horrible, grinding roar the earth fell back upon itself, leaving in its place a mountain of smoke. From the moment the mine went up my feelings changed. The crisis was over, and from that second I was cold, cool, and calculating.

I looked upon all that followed from the purely pictorial point of view, and even felt annoyed if a shell burst outside the range of my camera. Why couldn't Bosche put that shell a little nearer? It would make a better picture. And so my thoughts ran on.

The earth was down. I swung my camera round on to our own parapets. The engineers were swarming over the top, and streaming along the sky-line. Our guns redoubled their fire. The Germans then started H. E. Shrapnel began falling in the midst of our advancing men. I continued to turn the handle of my camera, viewing the whole attack through my view-finder, first swinging one way and then the other.

Then another signal rang out, and from the trenches immediately in front of me, our wonderful troops went over the top. What a picture it was! They went over as one man. I could see while I was exposing, that numbers were shot down before they reached the top of the parapet; others just the other side. They went across the ground in swarms, and marvel upon marvels, still smoking cigarettes. One man actually stopped in the middle of 'No Man's Land' to light up again.

The Germans had by now realised that the great attack had come. Shrapnel poured into our trenches with the object of keeping our supports from coming up. They had even got their "crumps" and high-explosive shrapnel into the middle of our boys before they were half-way across 'No Man's Land.' But still they kept on. At that moment my spool ran out. I hurriedly loaded up again, and putting the first priceless spool in my case, I gave it to my man in a dug-out to take care of, impressing upon him that he must not leave it under any circumstances. If anything unforeseen happened he was to take it back to Headquarters.

I rushed back to my machine again. Shells were exploding quite close to me. At least I was told so afterwards by an officer. But I was so occupied with my work that I was quite unconscious of their proximity. I began filming once more. The first lot of men, or rather the remainder of them, had disappeared in the haze and smoke, punctured by bursting shells. What was happening in the German lines I did not know. Other men were coming up and going over the top. The German machine-gun fire was not quite so deadly now, but our men suffered badly from shell-fire. On several occasions I noticed men run and take temporary cover in the shell-holes, but their ranks were being terribly thinned.

Still more went over, and still a stream of men were making for the mine crater; they then disappeared in the smoke. The noise was terrific. It was as if the earth were lifting bodily, and crashing against some immovable object. The very heavens seemed to be falling. Thousands of things were happening at the same moment. The mind could not begin to grasp the barest margin of it.

The German shells were crashing all round me. Dirt was being flung in my face, cutting it like whipcord. My only thought was whether any of it had struck my lens and made it dirty, for this would have spoiled my film. I gave a quick glance at it. It was quite all right.

Fearful fighting was taking place in the German trenches. The heavy rattle of machine-guns, the terrible din of exploding bombs, could be heard above the pandemonium. Our men had ceased to flow from our trenches. I crept to the top of the parapet, and looked towards the left of the village of Beaumont Hamel. Our guns were bursting on the other side of the village, but I could distinguish nothing else as to how things were going.

I asked an officer who was standing close by.

"God knows," he replied. "Everything over there is so mixed up. The General said this was the hardest part of the line to get through, and my word it seems like it, to look at our poor lads."

I could see them strewn all over the ground, swept down by the accursed machine-gun fire.

A quick succession of shell-bursts attracted my attention. Back to my camera position. Another lot of our men were going over the top. I began exposing, keeping them in my camera view all the time, as they were crossing, by revolving my tripod head.

Shell after shell crashed in the middle of them, leaving ghastly gaps, but other men quickly filled them up, passing through the smoke, and over the bodies of their comrades, as if there were no such thing as a shell in all the world. Another spool ran out, making the fourth since the attack started. I gave it in charge of my man, with the same instructions as before. I loaded again, and had just started exposing. Something attracted my attention on the extreme left. What it was I don't know. I ceased turning, but still holding the handle, I veered round the front of my camera. The next moment, with a shriek and a flash, a shell fell and exploded before I had time to take shelter. It was only a few feet away. What happened after I hardly know. There was the grinding crash of a bursting shell; something struck my tripod, the whole thing, camera and all, was flung against me. I clutched it and staggered back, holding it in my arms. I dragged it into a shrapnel-proof shelter, sat down and looked for the damage. A piece of the shell had struck the tripod and cut the legs clean in half, on one side, carrying about six inches of it away. The camera, thank heaven, was untouched.

Calling my man, we hastily found some pieces of wood, old telephone wire and string, and within an hour had improvised legs, rigid enough to continue taking scenes.

I again set up my camera. Our gun-fire was still terrible, but the Germans had shortened their range and were evidently putting a barrage on our men, who had presumably reached the enemy's front trenches.

Nobody knew anything definitely. Wounded men began to arrive. There was a rush for news.

"How are things going?" we asked.

"We have taken their first and second line," said one.

An officer passed on a stretcher.

"How are things going?"

"God knows," he said. "I believe we have got through their first line and part of the village, but don't know whether we shall be able to hold out; we have been thinned shockingly."

"Have you been successful?" he asked me.

"Yes, I've got the whole of the attack."

"Good man," he said.

First one rumour then another came through. There was nothing definite. The fighting over there was furious. I filmed various scenes of our wounded coming in over the parapet; then through the trenches. Lines of them were awaiting attention.

Scenes crowded upon me. Wounded and more wounded; men who a few hours before had leaped over the parapet full of life and vigour were now dribbling back. Some of them shattered and broken for life. But it was one of the most glorious charges ever made in the history of the world. These men had done their bit.

"Hullo," I said to one passing through on a stretcher, "got a 'blighty'?"

"Yes, sir," he said; "rather sure Blighty for me."

"And for me too," said another lad lying with him waiting attention, "I shan't be able to play footer any more. Look!" I followed the direction of his finger, and could see through the rough bandages that his foot had been taken completely off. Yet he was still cheerful, and smoking.

A great many asked me as they came through: "Was I in the picture, sir?" I had to say "yes" to them all, which pleased them immensely.

Still no definite news. The heavy firing continued. I noticed several of our wounded men lying in shell-holes in 'No Man's Land.' They were calling for assistance. Every time a Red Cross man attempted to get near them, a hidden German machine-gun fired. Several were killed whilst trying to bring in the wounded. The cries of one poor fellow attracted the attention of a trench-mortar man. He asked for a volunteer to go with him, and bring the poor fellow in. A man stepped forward, and together they climbed the parapet, and threaded their way through the barbed wire very slowly. Nearer and nearer they crept. We stood watching with bated breath. Would they reach him? Yes. At last! Then hastily binding up the injured man's wounds they picked him up between them, and with a run made for our parapet. The swine of a German blazed away at them with his machine-gun. But marvellous to relate neither of them were touched.

I filmed the rescue from the start to the finish, until they passed me in the trench, a mass of perspiration. Upon the back of one was the unconscious man he had rescued, but twenty minutes after these two had gone through hell to rescue him, the poor fellow died.

During the day those two men rescued twenty men in this fashion under heavy fire.

*   *   *   *   *

The day wore on. The success of the fighting swayed first this way, then that. The casualties mounted higher and higher. Men were coming back into our trenches maimed and broken; they all had different tales to tell. I passed along talking to and cheering our wonderful men as much as I could. And the Germans, to add to this ghastly whirlpool of horror, threw shell after shell into the dressing station, killing and wounding afresh the gallant lads who had gone "over the top" that morning. They seemed to know of this place and played upon it with a gloating, fiendish glee worthy only of unspeakable savages.

As I was passing one group of wounded, I ran against my doctor friend of the night before.

"Busy day for you?" I said.

"My word, yes," he replied. "They are coming faster than I can attend to them. I am just off to see P——. He's caught it badly."

"Serious?" I asked.

"Yes, rather; in the back. He's in the dug-out."

And the doctor rushed away. I followed him. P—— was lying there on a stretcher looking ghastly. The doctor was bending over him. Poor old chap. Only that morning he had hooked me out to film the sunken road scenes as full of life and hope as anyone could conceive. Now he was on his back, a broken wreck. In the trenches there were hundreds of cases as bad, or even worse, but they did not affect me. There were far too many for the mind to fully grasp their meaning. But down here in this dark dug-out, twenty feet below the earth, the sombre surroundings only illuminated by a guttering candle in a bottle, I was far more affected. It was natural though, for one always feels things more when someone one knows is concerned.

P—— was the first to speak.

"Hullo, old man," he said in a husky, low voice. "You've pulled through?"

"Yes," I replied. "But 'touchwood'! I'm so sorry. Anyway, you're all right for 'Blighty,'" and to cheer him up I continued in a bantering strain: "You knew how to manage it, eh? Jolly artful, you know." His face lighted up with a wan smile.

"Yes, Malins, rather a long 'Blighty,' I'm afraid."

Two stretcher-bearers came in at that moment to take him away. With difficulty they got him out of the trench, and grasping his hand I bade him good-bye.

"I'm glad you got our boys, Malins. I do so want to see that film," were his last words.

"I'll show it to you when I get back to England," I called after him, and then he disappeared.

The fighting was now beginning to die down. The remnants of four regiments were coming in. Each section was accumulating in spaces on their own. I realised that the roll-call was about to take place. I filmed them as they staggered forward and dropped down utterly worn out, body and soul. By an almost superhuman effort many of them staggered to their feet again, and formed themselves into an irregular line.

In one little space there were just two thin lines - all that was left of a glorious regiment (barely one hundred men). I filmed the scene as it unfolded itself. The sergeant stood there with note-book resting on the end of his rifle, repeatedly putting his pencil through names that were missing. This picture was one of the most wonderful, the most impressive that can be conceived. It ought to be painted and hung in all the picture galleries of the world, in all the schools and public buildings, and our children should be taught to regard it as the standard of man's self-sacrifice.

I stayed in the trenches until the following day, filming scene after scene of our wounded. I learned that nothing more was to be attempted until later, when fresh divisions were to be brought up. Knowing this I decided to leave this section of the trenches. But the ghastly scenes of which I was witness will always remain a hideous nightmare in my memory, though I thank God I had been spared to film such tremendous scenes of supreme heroism and sacrifice in the cause of freedom.

I got safely back through the trenches to ——, where Brigade H.Q.

told me of an urgent message from G.H.Q. I was to report as soon as possible. On my way I called on General ——, who was delighted to hear I had successfully filmed the attack, the record of which would show the world how gloriously our men had fought.

Reaching advanced G.H.Q. I reported myself. All were pleased to see me safe and sound, and to hear of my success. I was told that lively things were happening at La Boisselle. I heard also how successful our troops had been in other parts of the line. Fricourt and Mametz and a dozen other villages had fallen to our victorious troops. This news put new life into me. At La Boisselle they said we had pushed through, and fighting was still going on. I decided to leave for that district right away.

Passing through Albert, I halted the car at the top of Becourt Wood. From this point I had to walk. In the distance I could see hundreds of shells bursting, and guns were thundering out. I gave one camera to my orderly and another had the tripod. Taking the second camera myself, I started off. We threaded our way through the wood and out into the trenches. Shells were falling close by, but by hugging the parapet we got along fairly well.

The communication trench seemed interminable.

"Where the deuce am I?" I asked an officer in passing. "I want to get to our front trenches."

"You want to go the other way. This trench leads back to ——."

This was anything but cheering news. I had been walking for about an hour, always seeming to just miss the right turning. Truth to tell I had failed to provide myself with a trench map, and it was my first time in this section. The bursting shells were filling up the trenches, and I was becoming absolutely fogged. So, in sheer desperation - for the bombardment was getting more intense and I was afraid of losing pictures - I climbed on to the parapet to look round. What a scene of desolation. The first thing I saw was a dead German. That didn't help to cheer me up overmuch. Making a slight detour I stopped to fix the Hun front line if possible. Our own I could see. But no matter where I looked the Bosche line was apparently nonexistent. Yet our shells were smashing into the ground, which seemed to be absolutely empty.

I set up my camera and started to expose. While doing so I happened to glance down, for I must explain that I was on a slight mound. Which was the most surprised - the Bosche or myself - I do not know, for less than a hundred yards away was the German line. I stopped turning. Immediately I did so bullets came singing unpleasantly past my head. I dropped flat on the ground, which luckily for me was slightly protected by a ridge of earth. I dragged the camera down on top of me and, lying flat, the bullets whizzed by overhead. The Bosche must have thought he had got me, for in a few moments fire ceased. I wriggled towards the trench and dropped like a log into the bottom, dragging my camera after me. One of my men had followed, and seeing me drop, did the same. He came tumbling head first into the trench.

"That was a near squeak, sir," he said. "Yes, come on, they will probably start shelling us. Cut through here. I noticed some German prisoners coming this way. I must get them. Where's the other man? Keep him close up."

Reaching a trench through which the German prisoners were being led, I hurriedly fixed my camera and filmed them shambling in, holding their hands up, their nerves completely shattered by the intensity of our terrific bombardment. Some were covered with wounds, others were carrying our wounded Tommies in on stretchers. It was an extraordinary sight. Ten minutes before these men were doing their utmost to kill each other. Now, friend and foe were doing their best to help each other. Shells were dropping close by. One fell in the midst of a group of prisoners and, bursting, killed fourteen and wounded eleven. The others were marched on.

Whether I had been spotted or not, I do not know, but German shells were crumping unpleasantly near. I was just thinking of moving when another burst so close that it made me quickly decide. I looked round for my men. One was there; the other was missing.

"Get into a dug-out," I yelled. "Where is L——?"

"Don't know, sir," he said.

He dived into a dug-out at the first shell which burst near. At that moment another "crump" crashed down and exploded with a crunching roar, throwing a large quantity of earth all around me. One after another came over in quick succession.

"Where the devil is that fellow?" I said to ——. "He's got my aeroscope. When brother Fritz has smoothed down this little 'strafe' I will try and find him."

"He was in that section, sir, where Bosche crossed."

For over half an hour the crumping continued, then it practically ceased. The Bosche evidently thought he had distributed us to the four winds of heaven. I emerged from my shelter and hurriedly ran along the trench to find my man. He was nowhere to be found. Several dug-outs had been smashed in, and in one place the water in the trench was deep red with blood, and wading through this was anything but pleasant. At that moment a telephone man came up.

"Can you tell me, sir, if there is a machine-gun position hereabouts? I have been sent to run a wire." I was just replying when a crump came hurtling over.

"Duck," I yelled, and duck we did. I tried to cover the whole of my body under my steel helmet, and crouching low on the ground, the crump burst just on the parapet above, showering huge lumps of dirt which clattered upon us.

"You had better get out of this," I said, and suiting the action to the word I attempted to run, when another crump burst, this time in the traverse close behind. Well, which of us ran the fastest for cover I don't know, but I was a good second!

The non-appearance of my other man worried me. He was nowhere to be found. It occurred to me that as he did not find me on emerging from his dug-out, and as it was coming on to rain, he had returned to the car thinking he might find me there. Packing up my camera, therefore, I started off, passing more prisoners on the way. I promptly collared two of them to carry my tripod and camera, and as we proceeded I could not restrain a smile at the sight of two German prisoners hurrying along with my outfit, and a grinning Tommy with his inevitable cigarette between his lips, and a bayonet at the ready, coming up behind. It was too funny for words.

When I reached the car my lost man was not there. I enquired of several battle-police and stretcher-bearers if they had seen a man of his description wandering about, and carrying a leather case, but nobody had seen him. After having a sandwich, I decided to go again to the front line to find him. I could not leave him there. I must find out something definite. On my way down I made further enquiries, but without result. I searched around those trenches until I was soaked to the skin and fagged out, but not a trace of him could I discover; not even my camera or pieces of it. The only thing that could have happened, I thought, was that he had got into a dug-out, and the entrance had been blown in by heavy shell-fire.

Retracing my steps I examined several smashed dug-outs. It was impossible to even attempt to lift the rubble. With gloomy thoughts I returned again to the car, and on my journey back left instructions with various men to report anything found to the town major at —— I stayed the night in the vicinity in the hope of receiving news; but not a scrap came through. Again next day, and the next, I hunted the trenches, unsuccessfully, and finally I came to the conclusion that he had been killed and decided to post him as missing. I had arrived at this decision whilst resting on the grass at the top of Becourt Wood and was making a meal of bully and biscuits when, looking up, I saw what I took to be an apparition of my missing man walking along the road and carrying a black case. I could scarcely believe my eyes.

"Where the devil have you been?" I asked. "I was just on my way back to post you as missing. What has happened?"

"Well, sir, it was like this. When that shell burst I dived into a dug-out, and was quite all right. Then another shell burst and struck the entrance, smashing it in. I have been all this time trying to get out. Then I lost my way and - well, sir, here I am. But your camera case is spoilt." So ended his adventure.

Thinking that the films I had obtained of the Somme fighting should be given to the public as quickly as possible, I suggested to G.H.Q. - and they fully agreed - that I should return to England without delay. So packing up my belongings I returned to London next day.

Little time was lost in developing and printing the pictures, and the Military authorities, recognising what a splendid record they presented of "The Great Push," had copies prepared without delay for exhibition throughout the length and breadth of the land; in our Dependencies over seas, and in neutral countries. They were handled with wonderful celerity by Mr. Will Jury, a member of the War Office Committee, and put out through the business organisation over which he so ably presides. It is sufficient here to record the deep and abiding impression created by the appearance of the films on the screen. People crowded the theatres to see the pictures; thousands were turned away; and it has been estimated that the number of those who have seen these Official War Films must run into many millions.

The Somme Film has proved a mighty instrument in the service of recruiting; the newspapers still talk of its astounding realism, and it is generally admitted that the great kinematograph picture has done much to help the people of the British Empire to realise the wonderful spirit of our men in the face of almost insuperable difficulties; the splendid way in which our great citizen army has been organised; the vastness of the military machine we have created during the last two and a half years; and the immensity of the task which still faces us.

His Majesty the King has declared that "the public should see these pictures"; and Mr. Lloyd George, after witnessing a display of the film, sent forth the following thrilling message to the nation: "Be up and doing! See that this picture, which is in itself an epic of self-sacrifice and gallantry, reaches every one. Herald the deeds of our brave men to the ends of the earth. This is *your* duty."

A thrilling message truly, and I am proud indeed to think that I have been permitted to play my part in the taking and making of this wonderful film.

- CHAPTER 4 -

BLINDED ON THE SOMME

by Henry Gilbert Nobbs

HENRY GILBERT NOBBS was born in London in 1880. During the First World War, he served as a Captain in the London Rifle Brigade. In 1916 during the Somme Offensive, he led his company in an assault on the German trenches. In the close fighting he was shot through the head, and the bullet exited through his right eye, permanently blinding him. He lay in a shell-hole for two days, as the battle raged round him and eventually woke up in a German hospital. After his wounds were treated he was sent to a POW camp. His next of kin had already been informed of his death and had received a telegram of condolences from Buckingham Palace, and it was a month before they learned the shocking truth.

As a result of the severity of his injuries Captain Nobbs was repatriated to England where he composed this memoir of his experiences in the Great War. Nobbs later moved to Australia where, despite his handicap, he became a successful company director and a keen sports supporter. Originally published in 1922 as *On the Right of the British Line* this is the extraordinary autobiographical account of Henry Gilbert Nobbs an extraordinary man of surprising energy and one of life's enduring monuments to the human spirit.

This short extract commences with his vivid description of the advance through Leuze Wood and receiving the new operational order which order an advance "at any cost."

*   *   *   *   *

I HAD HARDLY CLOSED MY EYES WHEN A runner from headquarters came hurrying along the line, and was directed to where I was dozing at the bottom of a trench.

"Message from the C.O., sir, very urgent."

I signed the receipt and tore the envelope open. Good heavens! New operation orders! I was astounded. I looked again, hardly daring to believe my eyes. Sure enough, there was no mistake about it, three pages of closely written operation orders. The head-line seemed to be mocking me:

"Fresh operation orders, cancelling those issued this morning."

I read on: "You are to advance on through Leuze Wood, and attack from that part of the wood which forms the fourth side of the square-shaped trench, thus attacking the inside of the square; B Company taking the lower half, and C Company the upper half; A Company to be in support."

A cold shiver ran down my back. What a calamity! and after all the pains I had taken to work out the details of the attack, and that dreadful night spent in digging these trenches to jump off from. Every man knew what to do, and now at the eleventh hour the whole plan was altered.

I glanced again at the new orders:

"You are to be at the new place of assembly by 3.30 P.M.; zero hour is 4.45."

I looked at my watch - Great Scott! It was already 2.15; at 3 P.M. I must commence the advance through the wood.

The men had not yet commenced their dinners. What time was there? and how was it possible to sit down quietly and digest those three pages of new orders and understand their meaning? What time had I to make new plans and explain to each man his new task?

There was not a moment to be lost; I turned to my two runners:

"Dinners to be eaten at once. Platoon commanders wanted at the double."

I waited, and by and by the platoon commanders, Second Lieutenant Farman and Chislehirst, and Sergeants Blackwell and Barnes, came running along the top, snipers shooting at them as they ran along. They halted on the parados, saluting as they came up, and, still standing up, awaited orders, seemingly indifferent to the excellent target which they presented.

"Lie down flat," I ordered.

They did as I directed, their faces turned anxiously toward me, wondering what was up.

"New operation orders just arrived from headquarters; previous orders cancelled. We are to advance through the wood and attack from the inside of the square."

I hurriedly read the whole of the orders over to them, and they listened silently.

"Go back to your platoons. The men are to be dressed in battle order by 2.50 - it's now 2.30 - by 3 P.M. the platoons are to be closed up along the trench, and the leading platoon will enter the wood in single file, other platoons following."

As I glanced up I noticed their faces were pale; they were listening intently, but uttering no sound. They were receiving orders; they realised their responsibility, and they knew their duty.

The last paragraph was underlined. I hurriedly read it and looked up at them again:

"Just one more thing," I said. "These are my orders underlined:

"YOU MUST REACH YOUR OBJECTIVE AT ANY COST. IF DRIVEN BACK, YOU ARE TO MAKE A STAND AT THE EDGE OF THE WOOD, AND HOLD OUT TILL THE LAST MAN FALLS."

It sounded like a death sentence, a forecast of the hour of trial which we were to face. Only those who have received such orders on the field of battle can realise what it feels like.

In those few dramatic moments we counted our lives as lost. We recognised how desperate was our task. Success we might hope for; but failure we must pay the price of. We must fight till the last man falls - and yet we were merely civilian soldiers.

I looked into their faces; our eyes met. I understood; I could trust them; they could trust me.

"That's all; return to your platoons and prepare to move."

They had not uttered a word through all this; no words were necessary. They jumped to their feet; saluted as though we were back on Salisbury Plain, and the next moment ran along the parados to their platoons.

I watched them, and saw them kneel down on the top of their trench, indifferent to the snipers' bullets whistling about their heads, hurriedly explaining the situation to their men.

By 3 p.m. the men were ready and had closed along the trench to the wood.

The movement had been seen by the enemy, and a terrific burst of firing commenced; although, at the time I could not see what effect it was having.

I waited several minutes, but there was no further movement along the trench to indicate that the first platoon had entered the wood. I sent forward the message, "Carry on," but still no movement resulted.

At last, feeling something was wrong and unable to restrain my impatience any longer, I jumped out of the trench and ran along the parados.

What I saw there appalled me for the moment; the wood in front of me was filled with bursting shells; a continuous pr-r-r-r seemed to be moving backward and forward, and bullets were whistling in all directions.

Good God! What a hell! No wonder the men hesitated! What was to be done? My orders left me no alternative. I must advance through the wood. My brain kept repeating the words, "At any cost!" What a cost it would be to enter that hell! It was now, or never!

We were hesitating; something must be done, and done quickly. I looked at Farman, and I knew I could count on him.

The next moment I leaped into a newly made shell-hole, about five yards in the wood; called upon Farman to follow, and a moment later he came jumping after.

The noise was terrific. We yelled at the top of our voices for the next man to follow.

The next man to take the leap was the company sergeant-major. A piece of shell struck him in the side, and he rolled over on the ground, clutching at his tunic.

Again we yelled for the men to come along; and one by one they took the leap.

When six of us were in the shell-hole it was time for us to empty it to make room for others. Farman and I took it in turns to lead the way, and this process went on through the wood, leaping from hole to hole, and yelling at the top of our lungs for the others to follow us.

By this time the scene inside the wood was indescribable. Machine-gun bullets were spraying backward and forward; 6-inch shells were exploding in all directions; and the din was intensified by the crashing of trees uprooted by the explosions, and the dull thud of the missiles striking the ground.

Through the dull light of that filthy wood we frequently cast an anxious glance towards the red rockets being sent up from the German lines, directing the fire of their artillery towards us.

Sometimes, in leaping forward, we would land beside the dead and mutilated carcass of a German soldier who had fallen a week before. It was ghastly, terrible; and the millions of flies sucking at his open wounds would swarm about us, seemingly in a buzz of anger at our disturbance. But sickly and ghastly as the scene was, farther and farther into this exaggerated hell we must go.

By this time the cries of the wounded added to the terrors of the scene. Each time we jumped into a shell-hole, we turned to watch the men leap in. Each time it seemed that a new face appeared, and the absence of those who had jumped into the last shell-hole was only too significant.

But, undaunted by their falling comrades, each man, in his turn, leaped forward and would lie gasping for breath until his turn came for another effort.

Farman was the first to speak. It was his turn to take the next leap:

"I don't think it really matters. There's a hole about thirty yards away; I think I'll go straight for that."

He got up and walked leisurely across, as though inviting the death which seemed inevitable. He stopped at the shell-hole, and for a moment seemed to be looking down undecided whether to jump in or not.

I shouted at him:

"Don't be a damned fool; jump!"

The next moment a shell burst between us, and I fell back into the shell-hole. When I again looked out and my eyes could penetrate the smoke, I saw no sign of Farman. I yelled, and to my intense relief I saw his head appear. He was safe!

Again and again the last paragraph of my orders seemed to be blazing in front of me, and like a hidden hand from that dark inferno of horrors, kept beckoning me forward, "AT ANY COST! AT ANY COST!"

Yes; this must be the end; but it's hell to die in a wood.

The men used to call it Lousy Wood. What do they call it now? They were brave fellows; and they were only civilian soldiers, too! They used to be volunteers once. People would laugh, and call them Saturday afternoon soldiers.

Reviews in Hyde Park used to be a joke, and the comic papers caricatured these men, and used them as material for their jests.

They were only Territorials! That man, panting hard at the bottom of the shell-hole, and still clutching at his rifle, is a bank clerk; that man who fell at the last jump, with his stomach ripped up, was a solicitor's clerk.

Look at the others. Their faces are pale; their eyes are bulging. But they are the same faces one used to see in Cornhill and Threadneedle Street.

Yes, they are only Territorials! But here in this filthy wood they are damned proud of it.

And what is taking place in England to-day?

Is it really true that while all this is going on in Leuze Wood, orchestras are playing sweet music in brilliantly lighted restaurants in London - while a gluttonous crowd eat of the fat of the land? Is it really true that women in England are dressing more extravagantly than ever? Is it really true that some men in England are unable or unwilling to share the nation's peril - are even threatening to strike?

No! No! Do not let us think that this is the true picture of England. If it is, then, Territorials, let us die in Leuze Wood!

*   *   *   *   *

Joy! The last leap I took landed me in a trench, and I found to my great relief that it was the lower part of the square which ran through the wood. A few yards along this trench it emerged into the open, where it was in possession of the Germans.

Farman and I sat down, side by side, breathing heavily from our exertions.

"That was hell, Farman," I said, hardly daring to trust my voice.

"Awful!"

"I hope the men are still following."

"Those that are left."

"Have a cigarette; it will buck the men up to see us smoking."

"Thanks, I will, though I'm as dry as a bone."

"Save your water; we've still got the attack to do. We've got an hour yet; that will give the men time to recover."

By this time, one by one, the men began to jump into the trench. As the men arrived, their faces pale and eyes started, we called them by name. They looked up and smiled with relief at seeing us sitting there, side by side. They recognised that the last jump had been made, and for the time being, at any rate, they were safe.

We had started through the wood, about one hundred and thirty strong, and barely eighty mustered for the final attack.

Some men of C Company appeared, threading their way along the trench. Farther in the wood, the commander, Lieutenant Barton, came up to arrange details for the attack.

"You got your new orders in time, then," I remarked.

"Just in time. It's hell, isn't it? I've lost heavily already, and we've still got to go over the top."

"I've got orders to take half the battalion bombers from you; where are they?"

"I would like to keep them; there are not many left, and they are badly broken up - been fighting all night."

"All right, you keep them. I'm going to form up between here and that broken tree. Will you form up farther to the left?"

"All right. Well, I'll be off; cheer oh! old chap."

"Good-bye, Barton. Good luck!"

I never saw Barton again! I heard some months afterwards that he fell, riddled with machine-gun bullets whilst leading his men into the subsequent attack.

"Pass the word for No. 8 Platoon commander," I ordered, wishing to ascertain if the last platoon had arrived.

A young sergeant came up at the double, and saluted.

"I am in command, sir."

His tone and manner inspired me immensely. Notwithstanding all the danger we had passed through, he seemed to be full of ginger and pride at finding himself in command of the platoon.

"Where is Mr. Chislehirst, then?" I asked.

"Wounded, sir, in the wood; shot through the chest. The last I saw of him he was giving another wounded man a drink from his water-bottle."

"All right; do you understand your orders?"

"Yes, sir, quite."

"Return to your platoon, and await orders to form up."

He saluted and doubled back to his men. I forget his name, but he was a fine fellow, that sergeant; quite cool, and evidently pleased at his new responsibility.

So poor old Chislehirst was hit; fine fellow; very young, only about twenty; good company in the mess; reliable in the field. Just like him to give his water-bottle to someone else when he could go no farther.

Farman was my only subaltern left. Suddenly he gripped my arm and pointed into the wood:

"Look over there. Who are those fellows creeping along that trench?"

I looked in the direction he was pointing, and there, to my astonishment, on the very ground just vacated by C Company, about a dozen figures in bluish grey were creeping along a shallow trench. I thought at first they were coming in to surrender; but they made no signs, but were evidently making the best of cover.

What were they up to? There were only about 12 of them, and I had between 70 and 80 men. For such a small number to come out alone and attack us seemed absurd, and I waited, expecting them to throw up their hands and come in. Perhaps they thought they had not been seen. I picked up a rifle, and taking aim, fired at the last man but one; I missed.

Still they kept creeping on. I fired a second time at the same man, and he dropped. The thing didn't seem real, seeing those heads bobbing along a trench; I felt for a moment as though I were shooting rabbits.

The next moment I realised their object. By this time they had worked well round my flanks. They were evidently a few daring men, who were trying to creep up unnoticed, with the intention of throwing bombs while we were in a congested area, occupied in forming up for the attack. A daring ruse, but a clever one; for a dozen men throwing bombs at close quarters could wipe us off the map, or, at any rate, could do enough damage by shock action of this kind to prevent our attack starting.

I dared not give any order to fire for fear of hitting the men of C Company. The situation was desperate. I had no time to spare, for zero hour was close at hand. The same thoughts were running through Farman's mind.

"Shall I have a go at them?" he said.

"Yes; form up your platoon, and stick them with the bayonet; then join the attack as a fourth wave."

I watched Farman and his platoon with bayonets fixed, creeping on all fours towards the German bombers. That was the last I saw of them, as it was within 10 minutes of zero hour, and we were not yet in battle formation.

I heard afterwards that they did the job well. But to part with the platoon and my only remaining officer at this critical moment was a great loss to me; for I could not count upon them in the attack for which I had now only three platoons left - about sixty men.

Half my strength had gone, and the real attack had not yet begun. I sent for the remaining platoon commanders and explained the situation:

"No. 6 Platoon will now become the first wave. Form up and extend along the edge of the wood and await my signal to advance into the open. No. 7 Platoon, form up immediately in rear; and No. 8 Platoon, assemble in the trench close up. Bombing section of No. 6 will proceed along the trench parallel with the advance, bombing it out as they go along."

The men formed up. The minutes seemed to be like hours. We were facing the inside of the square trench, which was a mass of shell-holes, and as though anticipating our intention, shells were bursting and bullets whistling on all sides.

How peaceful England must be at this moment; how pretty the villages! And how wicked this hell seemed in front of us! And these were the men of England - nice chaps, only Territorials.

One used to meet them in the city every day. Some were awful nuts. See them at lunch; watch them pouring out of Liverpool Street Station between 9 and 10 o'clock in the morning, with newspaper and walking-stick; see them in the banks, bending over ledgers. You could hardly believe it; but these were the same men.

They were not very trim just now; their hands were grimy as they clutched at their rifles, undaunted by the terrors they have already passed through and the sight of their fallen comrades left groaning in the wood.

There they are, extended and lying flat on the ground, waiting further orders. They have come through one hell by the skin of their teeth, and are patiently looking into another hell; their lives were counted by minutes, these office men. But their eyes were fixed on the far side of the square trench which was to be their objective; unless by God's will, and for the sake of England, they found an earlier one.

London men! Some may call you "only Territorials." Training has been your hobby; but fighting was never your profession.

What will England think of this? England may never know.

Who ever heard of Leuze Wood before? If a man is killed in England there is an inquest. People read about it in the papers.

Are the people left behind in England suffering hardships uncomplainingly, and gritting their teeth like you are? You are only getting a bob a day. England needs you; you are masters. Why don't you strike at this critical moment?

No, my lads; you are made of different stuff. You are men! There are those in England this day who work for England's cause; there are others who are enriching themselves by your absence; there are homes which will feel your sacrifice.

You have seen the wasted homes and the ghastly outrages in France; and between that picture and the green fields of England you must make your stand; those in England will depend upon you this day.

Zero hour is at hand. Agonies, mutilation, and death are within a few yards of you. There will be no pictures of your deeds; there are no flags or trumpets to inspire you; you are lying on the dirty ground on the edge of Leuze Wood, with hell in front of you, and hell behind you - hell in those trenches on the left, hell in those trenches on the right.

One more minute and you will stand up and walk into it. My lads! It's for England!

*   *   *   *   *

At last the thunder of our guns towards the German lines confirmed the hour. Zero hour had arrived; the barrage had begun.

"No. 6 Platoon will advance."

The front line jumped up and walked into the open. Wonderful! Steady as a rock! The line was perfect.

On the left the front line of C Company has also emerged from the wood; the bombers of No. 6 Platoon disappeared along the mystery trench.

The tut-ut-ut-ut of machine-guns developed from several parts of the square, while the crack of rifles increased in intensity.

No. 7 Platoon jumped up and advanced into the open, followed by the third wave.

I extended my runners and followed.

What followed next beggars description. As I write these lines my hand hesitates to describe the hell that was let loose upon those men. No eye but mine could take in the picture so completely.

Will the world ever know what these men faced and fought against - these men of the City of London? Not unless I tell it, for I alone saw all that happened that day; and my hand alone, weak and incapable though it feels, is the only one that can do it.

Barely had I emerged from the wood with my ten runners when a perfect hurricane of shells were hurled at us, machine-guns from several points spraying their deadly fire backward and forward, dropping men like corn before the reaper. From all three sides of the square a hurricane of fire was poured into the centre of the square upon us, as we emerged from the wood.

In far less time than it takes to record it, the attacking waves became a mere sprinkling of men. They went on for a yard or two, and then all seemed to vanish; and even my runners, whom I had extended into line, were dropping fast.

The situation was critical, desperate. Fearful lest the attack should fail, I ran forward, and collecting men here and there from shell-holes where some had taken refuge, I formed them into a fresh firing-line, and once more we pressed forward.

Again and again the line was thinned; and again the survivors, undaunted and unbeaten, reformed and pressed forward.

Men laughed, men cried in the desperation of the moment. We were grappling with death; we were dodging it, cheating it; we were mad, blindly hysterical. What did anything matter? Farther and farther into the inferno we must press, at any cost, at any cost; leaping, jumping, rushing, we went from shell-hole to shell-hole; and still the fire continued with unrelenting fury.

I jumped into a shell-hole, and found myself within ten yards of my objective. My three remaining runners jumped in alongside of me. They were Arnold, Dobson, and Wilkinson.

Arnold was done for! He looked up at me with eyes staring and face blanched, and panted out that he could go no farther, and I realised that

I could count on him no more. I glanced to the left, just in time to see three Germans riot five yards away, and one after the other jump from a shell-hole which formed a sort of bay to their trench, and run away.

Wishing to save the ammunition in my revolver for the hand-to-hand scuffle which seemed imminent, I seized the rifle of Arnold and fired. I missed all three; my hand was shaky.

What was I to do next? The company on my left had disappeared; the trench just in front of me was occupied by the Bodies. I had with me three runners, one of whom was helpless, and in the next shell-hole about six men, the sole survivors of my company.

Where were the supports? Anxiously I glanced back toward the wood; why did they not come?

Poor fellows, I did not know it at the time, but the hand of death had dealt with them even more heavily in the wood than it had with us.

My position was desperate. I could not retire. My orders were imperative: "You must reach your objective at any cost." I must get there somehow. But even if we got there, how long could I hope to hold out with such a handful of men?

Immediate support I must have; I must take risks. I turned to brave Dobson and Wilkinson:

"Message to the supports: 'Send me two platoons quickly; position critical.'"

Without a moment's hesitation they jumped up and darted off with the message which might save the day.

Dobson fell before he had gone two yards; three paces farther on I saw Wilkinson, the pet of the company, turn suddenly round and fall on the ground, clutching at his breast. All hope for the supports was gone.

At this moment the bombing section, which by this time had cleared the mystery trench, arrived on the right of the objective; and to my delirious joy, I noticed the Germans in the trench in front of me running away along the trench.

It was now, or never! We must charge over that strip of land and finish them with the bayonet. A moment's hesitation and the tables might again be turned, and all would be lost. The trench in front must be taken by assault; it must be done. There were six or seven of us left, and we must do it.

I yelled to the men:

"Get ready to charge, they are running. Come on! Come on!"

I jumped out of the shell-hole, and they followed me. Once again I was mad. I saw nothing, I heard nothing; I wanted to kill! kill!

Pf-ung!

Oh! My God! I was hit in the head! I was blind!

CHAPTER 5

AN AMERICAN IN THE BRITISH ARMY

by Robert Derby Holmes

THIS ACCOUNT BY ROBERT DERBY HOLMES provides an highly unusual perspective on the Battle of the Somme. Robert Derby Holmes was an American who volunteered to fight in the ranks of the British Army and saw a great deal of action during the Great War. Like Gilbert Nobbs he later had the misfortune to be wounded but he was able to make a full recovery and produced a highly readable account of his war which was published under the title *A Yankee In the Trenches*.

After the failure of the initial phase of the battle, the fight lingered on into November before the battle was closed down. One innovation that did appear on the battlefield was the introduction of the tank and Derby Holmes was on the spot to witness the first introduction to combat.

*   *   *   *   *

WE HAD BEEN ON MILL STREET A DAY and a night when an order came for our company to move up to the second line and to be ready to go over the top the next day. At first there was the usual grousing, as there seemed to be no reason why our company should be picked from the whole battalion. We soon learned that all hands were going over, and after that we felt better.

We got our equipment on and started up to the second line. It was right here that I got my first dose of real honest-to-goodness modern war. The "Big Push" had been on all summer, and the whole of the Somme district was battered and smashed.

Going up from Mill Street there were no communication trenches. We were right out in the open, exposed to rifle and machine-gun fire and to shrapnel, and the Boches were fairly raining it in on the territory they had been pushed back from and of which they had the range to an inch. We went up under that steady fire for a full hour. The casualties were heavy, and the galling part of it was that we couldn't hurry, it was so dark. Every time a shell burst overhead and the shrapnel pattered in the dirt all about, I kissed myself good-by and thought of the baked beans at home. Men kept falling, and I wished I hadn't enlisted.

When we finally got up to the trench, believe me, we didn't need any orders to get in. We relieved the Black Watch, and they encouraged us by telling us they had lost over half their men in that trench, and that Fritz kept a constant fire on it. They didn't need to tell us. The big boys were coming over all the time.

The dead here were enough to give you the horrors. I had never seen so many before and never saw so many afterwards in one place. They were all over the place, both Germans and our own men. And in all states of mutilation and decomposition.

There were arms and legs sticking out of the trench sides. You could tell their nationality by the uniforms. The Scotch predominated. And their dead lay in the trenches and outside and hanging over the edges. I think it was here that I first got the real meaning of that old quotation about the curse of a dead man's eye. With so many lying about, there were always eyes staring at you.

Sometimes a particularly wide-staring corpse would seem to follow you with his gaze, like one of these posters with the pointing finger that they use to advertise Liberty Bonds. We would cover them up or turn them over. Here and there one would have a scornful death smile on his lips, as though he were laughing at the folly of the whole thing.

The stench here was appalling. That frightful, sickening smell that strikes one in the face like something tangible. Ugh! I immediately grew dizzy and faint and had a mad desire to run. I think if I hadn't been a non-com with a certain small amount of responsibility to live up to, I should have gone crazy.

I managed to pull myself together and placed my men as comfortably as possible. The Germans were five hundred yards away, and there was but little danger of an attack, so comparatively few had to "stand to." The rest took to the shelters.

I found a little two-man shelter that everybody else had avoided and crawled in. I crowded up against a man in there and spoke to him. He didn't answer and then suddenly I became aware of a stench more powerful than ordinary. I put out my hand and thrust it into a slimy, cold mess. I had found a dead German with a gaping, putrefying wound in his abdomen. I crawled out of that shelter, gagging and retching. This time I simply couldn't smother my impulse to run, and run I did, into the next traverse, where I sank weak and faint on the fire step. I sat there the rest of the night, regardless of shells, my mind milling wildly on the problem of war and the reason thereof and cursing myself for a fool.

It was very early in the morning when Wells shook me up with, "Hi sye, Darby, wot the blinkin' blazes is that noise?"

We listened, and away from the rear came a tremendous whirring, burring, rumbling buzz, like a swarm of giant bees. I thought of everything from a Zeppelin to a donkey engine but couldn't make it out. Blofeld ran around the corner of a traverse and told us to get the men out. He didn't know what was coming and wasn't taking any chances.

It was getting a little light though heavily misty. We waited, and then out of the gray blanket of fog waddled the great steel monsters that we were to know afterwards as the "tanks." I shall never forget it.

In the half darkness they looked twice as big as they really were. They lurched forward, slow, clumsy but irresistible, nosing down into shell holes and out, crushing the unburied dead, sliding over mere trenches as though they did not exist.

There were five in all. One passed directly over us. We scuttled out of the way, and the men let go a cheer. For we knew that here was something that could and would win battles.

The tanks were an absolutely new thing to us. Their secret had been guarded so carefully even in our own army that our battalion had heard nothing of them.

But we didn't need to be told that they would be effective. One look was enough to convince us. Later it convinced Fritzie.

*   *   *   *   *

The tanks passed beyond us and half-way up to the first line and stopped. Trapdoors in the decks opened, and the crews poured out and began to pile sandbags in front of the machines so that when day broke fully and the mists lifted, the enemy could not see what had been brought up in the night.

Day dawned, and a frisky little breeze from the west scattered the fog and swept the sky clean. There wasn't a cloud by eight o'clock. The sun shone bright, and we cursed it, for if it had been rainy the attack would not have been made.

We made the usual last preparations that morning, such as writing letters and delivering farewell messages; and the latest rooks made their wills in the little blanks provided for the purpose in the back of the pay books. We judged from the number of dead and the evident punishment other divisions had taken there that the chances of coming back would be slim. Around nine o'clock Captain Green gave us a little talk that confirmed our suspicions that the day was to be a hard one.

He said, as nearly as I can remember:

"Lads, I want to tell you that there is to be a most important battle - one of the most important in the whole war. High Wood out there commands a view of the whole of this part of the Somme and is most valuable. There are estimated to be about ten thousand Germans in that wood and in the surrounding supports. The positions are mostly of concrete with hundreds of machine guns and field artillery. Our heavies have for some reason made no impression on them, and regiment after regiment has attempted to take the woods and failed with heavy losses. Now it is up to the 47th Division to do the seemingly impossible. Zero is at eleven. We go over then. The best of luck and God bless you."

We were all feeling pretty sour on the world when the sky pilot came along and cheered us up.

He was a good little man, that chaplain, brave as they make 'em. He always went over the top with us and was in the thick of the fighting, and he had the military cross for bravery. He passed down the line, giving us a slap on the back or a hand grip and started us singing. No gospel hymns either, but any old rollicking, good-natured song that he happened to think of that would loosen things up and relieve the tension.

Somehow he made you feel that you wouldn't mind going to hell if he was along, and you knew that he'd be willing to come if he could do any good. A good little man! Peace to his ashes.

At ten o'clock things busted loose, and the most intense bombardment ever known in warfare up to that time began. Thousands of guns, both French and English, in fact every available gun within a radius of fifteen miles, poured it in. In the Bedlamitish din and roar it was impossible to hear the next man unless he put his mouth up close to your ear and yelled.

My ear drums ached, and I thought I should go insane if the racket didn't stop. I was frightfully nervous and scared, but tried not to show it. An officer or a non-com must conceal his nervousness, though he be dying with fright.

The faces of the men were hard-set and pale. Some of them looked positively green. They smoked fag after fag, lighting the new ones on the butts.

All through the bombardment Fritz was comparatively quiet. He was saving all his for the time when we should come over. Probably, too, he was holed up to a large extent in his concrete dug-outs. I looked over the top once or twice and wondered if I, too, would be lying there unburied with the rats and maggots gnawing me into an unrecognizable mass. There were moments in that hour from ten to eleven when I was distinctly sorry for myself.

The time, strangely enough, went fast - as it probably does with a condemned man in his last hour. At zero minus ten the word went down the line "Ten to go" and we got to the better positions of the trench and secured our footing on the side of the parapet to make our climb over when the signal came. Some of the men gave their bayonets a last fond rub, and I looked to my bolt action to see that it worked well. I had ten rounds in the magazine, and I didn't intend to rely too much on the bayonet. At a few seconds of eleven I looked at my wrist watch and was afflicted again with that empty feeling in the solar plexus. Then the whistles shrilled; I blew mine, and over we went.

To a disinterested spectator who was far enough up in the air to be out of range it must have been a wonderful spectacle to see those thousands of men go over, wave after wave.

The terrain was level out to the point where the little hill of High Wood rose covered with the splintered poles of what had once been a forest. This position and the supports to the left and rear of it began to fairly belch machine-gun and shell fire. If Fritz had been quiet before, he gave us all he had now.

Our battalion went over from the second trench, and we got the cream of it.

The tanks were just ahead of us and lumbered along in an imposing row. They lurched down into deep craters and out again, tipped and reeled and listed, and sometimes seemed as though they must upset; but they came up each time and went on and on. And how slow they did seem to move! Lord, I thought we should never cover that five or six hundred yards.

The tank machine guns were spitting fire over the heads of our first wave, and their Hotchkiss guns were rattling. A beautiful creeping barrage preceded us. Row after row of shells burst at just the right distance ahead, spewing gobs of smoke and flashes of flame, made thin by the bright sunlight. Half a dozen airplanes circled like dragonflies up there in the blue.

There was a tank just ahead of me. I got behind it. And marched there. Slow! God, how slow! Anyhow, it kept off the machine-gun bullets, but not, the shrapnel. It was breaking over us in clouds. I felt the stunning patter of the fragments on my tin hat, cringed under it, and wondered vaguely why it didn't do me in.

Men in the front wave were going down like tenpins. Off there diagonally to the right and forward I glimpsed a blinding burst, and as much as a whole platoon went down.

Around me men were dropping all the time - men I knew. I saw Dolbsie clawing at his throat as he reeled forward, falling. I saw Vickers double up, drop his rifle, and somersault, hanging on to his abdomen.

A hundred yards away, to the right, an officer walked backwards with an automatic pistol balanced on his finger, smiling, pulling his men along like a drum major. A shell or something hit him. He disappeared in a welter of blood and half a dozen of the front file fell with him.

I thought we must be nearly there and sneaked a look around the edge of the tank. A traversing machine gun raked the mud, throwing up handfuls, and I heard the gruff "row, row" of flattened bullets as they ricocheted off the steel armour. I ducked back, and on we went.

Slow! Slow! I found myself planning what I would do when I got to the front trenches - if we ever did. There would be a grand rumpus, and I would click a dozen or more.

And then we arrived.

I don't suppose that trip across 'No Man's Land' behind the tanks took over five minutes, but it seemed like an hour.

At the end of it my participation in the Battle of High Wood ended. No, I wasn't wounded. But when we reached the Boche front trenches a strange thing happened. There was no fight worth mentioning. The tanks stopped over the trenches and blazed away right and left with their all-around traverse.

A few Boches ran out and threw silly little bombs at the monsters. The tanks, noses in air, moved slowly on. And then the Graybacks swarmed up out of shelters and dug-outs, literally in hundreds, and held up their hands, whining "Mercy, kamarad."

We took prisoners by platoons. Blofeld grabbed me and turned over a gang of thirty to me. We searched them rapidly, cut their suspenders and belts, and I started to the rear with them. They seemed glad to go. So was I.

As we hurried back over the five hundred yards that had been 'No Man's Land' and was now British ground, I looked back and saw the irresistible tanks smashing their way through the tree stumps of High Wood, still spitting death and destruction in three directions.

Going back we were under almost as heavy fire as we had been coming up. When we were about half-way across, shrapnel burst directly over our party and seven of the prisoners were killed and half a dozen wounded. I myself was unscratched. I stuck my hand inside my tunic and patted Dinky on the back, sent up a prayer for some more luck like that, and carried on.

After getting my prisoners back to the rear, I came up again but couldn't find my battalion. I threw in with a battalion of Australians and was with them for twenty-four hours.

When I found my chaps again, the Battle of High Wood was pretty well over. Our company for some reason had suffered very few casualties, less than twenty-nine. Company B, however, had been practically wiped out, losing all but thirteen men out of two hundred. The other two companies had less than one hundred casualties. We had lost about a third of our strength. It is a living wonder to me that any of us came through.

I don't believe any of us would have if it hadn't been for the tanks.

The net result of the Battle of High Wood was that our troops carried on for nearly two miles beyond the position to be taken. They had to fall back but held the wood and the heights. Three of the tanks were stalled in the farther edge of the woods - out of fuel - and remained there for three days unharmed under the fire of the German guns.

Eventually some one ventured out and got some juice into them, and they returned to our lines. The tanks had proved themselves, not only as effective fighting machines, but as destroyers of German morale.

*   *   *   *   *

For weeks after our first introduction to the tanks they were the chief topic of conversation in our battalion. And, notwithstanding the fact that we had seen the monsters go into action, had seen what they did and the effect they had on the Boche, the details of their building and of their mechanism remained a mystery for a long time.

For weeks about all we knew about them was what we gathered from their appearance as they reeled along, camouflaged with browns and yellows like great toads, and that they were named with quaint names like "Crème de Menthe" and "Diplodocus."

Eventually I met with a member of the crews who had manned the tanks at the Battle of High Wood, and I obtained from him a description of some of his sensations. It was a thing we had all wondered about, - how the men inside felt as they went over.

My tanker was a young fellow not over twenty-five, a machine gunner, and in a little *estaminet*, over a glass of citron and soda, he told me of his first battle.

"Before we went in," he said, "I was a little bit uncertain as to how we were coming out. We had tried the old boats out and had given them every reasonable test. We knew how much they would stand in the way of shells on top and in the way of bombs or mines underneath. Still there was all the difference between rehearsal and the actual going on the stage.

"When we crawled in through the trapdoor for the first time over, the shut-up feeling got me. I'd felt it before but not that way. I got to imagining what would happen if we got stalled somewhere in the Boche lines, and they built a fire around us. That was natural, because it's hot inside a tank at the best. You mustn't smoke either. I hadn't minded that in rehearsal, but in action I was crazy for a fag.

"We went across, you remember, at eleven, and the sun was shining bright. We were parboiled before we started, and when we got going good it was like a Turkish bath. I was stripped to the waist and was dripping. Besides that, when we begun to give 'em hell, the place filled with gas, and it was stifling. The old boat pitched a good deal going into shell holes, and it was all a man could do to keep his station. I put my nose up to my loophole to get air, but only once. The machine-gun bullets were simply rattling on our hide. Tock, tock, tock they kept drumming. The first shell that hit us must have been head on and a direct hit. There was a terrific crash, and the old girl shook all over, - seemed to pause a little even. But no harm was done. After that we breathed easier. We hadn't been quite sure that the Boche shells wouldn't do us in.

"By the time we got to the Boche trenches, we knew he hadn't anything that could hurt us. We just sat and raked him and laughed and wished it was over, so we could get the air."

I had already seen the effect of the tanks on the Germans. The batch of prisoners who had been turned over to me seemed dazed. One who spoke English said in a quavering voice:

"Gott in Himmel, Kamarad, how could one endure? These things are not human. They are not fair."

That "fair" thing made a hit with me after going against tear gas and hearing about liquid fire and such things.

The great number of the prisoners we took at High Wood were very scared looking at first and very surly. They apparently expected to be badly treated and perhaps tortured. They were tractable enough for the most part. But they needed watching, and they got it from me, as I had heard much of the treachery of the Boche prisoners.

On the way to the rear with my bunch, I ran into a little episode which showed the foolishness of trusting a German, - particularly an officer.

I was herding my lot along when we came up with about twelve in charge of a young fellow from a Leicester regiment. He was a private, and as most of his noncommissioned officers had been put out of action, he was acting corporal. We were walking together behind the prisoners, swapping notes on the fight, when one of his stopped, and no amount of coaxing would induce him to go any farther. He was an officer, of what rank I don't know, but judging from his age probably a lieutenant.

Finally Crane - that was the Leicester chap - went up to the officer, threatened him with his bayonet, and let him know that he was due for the cold steel if he didn't get up and hike.

Whereupon Mr. Fritz pulled an automatic from under his coat - he evidently had not been carefully searched - and aimed it at Crane. Crane dove at him and grabbed his wrist, but was too late. The gun went off and tore away Crane's right cheek. He didn't go down, however, and before I could get in without danger to Crane, he polished off the officer on the spot.

The prisoners looked almost pleased. I suppose they knew the officer too well. I bandaged Crane and offered to take his prisoners in, but he insisted upon carrying on. He got very weak from loss of blood after a bit, and I had two of the Boches carry him to the nearest dressing station, where they took care of him. I have often wondered whether the poor chap "clicked" it.

Eventually I got my batch of prisoners back to headquarters and turned them over. I want to say a word right here as to the treatment of the German prisoners by the British. In spite of the verified stories of the brutality shown to the Allied prisoners by the Hun, the English and French have too much humanity to retaliate. Time and again I have seen British soldiers who were bringing in Germans stop and spend their own scanty pocket money for their captives' comfort. I have done it myself.

Almost inevitably the Boche prisoners were expecting harsh treatment. I found several who said that they had been told by their officers that they would be skinned alive if they surrendered to the English. They believed it, and you could hardly blame the poor devils for being scared.

Whenever we were taking prisoners back, we always, unless we were in too much of a hurry, took them to the nearest canteen run by the Y.M.C.A. or by one of the artillery companies, and here we would buy English or American fags. And believe me, they liked them. Any one who has smoked the tobacco issued to the German army could almost understand a soldier surrendering just to get away from it.

Usually, too, we bought bread and sweets, if we could stand the price. The Heinies would bolt the food down as though they were half starved. And it was perfectly clear from the way they went after the luxuries that they got little more than the hard necessities of army fare.

At the Battle of High Wood the prisoners we took ran largely to very young fellows and to men of fifty or over. Some of the youngsters said they were only seventeen and they looked not over fifteen. Many of them had never shaved.

I think the sight of those war-worn boys, haggard and hard, already touched with cruelty and blood lust, brought home to me closer than ever before what a hellish thing war is, and how keenly Germany must be suffering, along with the rest of us.

- CHAPTER 6 -

A FIELD BATTERY ON THE SOMME

by C. A. Rose

THE ARTILLERY WAS THE WAR WINNING element which shaped the reality of combat on the Western front from 1914-1918. However there are surprisingly few surviving in-depth accounts by the men who actually served the guns. However, we are fortunate that artilleryman C. A. Rose produced a vivid and detailed account of the fighting in France and the reality of the artillery at the front fighting in a war. The dangerous lives of the Forward Observation Officer and his team of signallers who operated in the front line trenches are highlighted in this detailed and highly readable memoir which was first published in 1919 under the title *Three Years In France with the Guns - Episodes In the Life of a Field Battery.*

Rose saw service on both 18-pounder field guns and also the heavier howitzers which provided the devastating power which eventually broke the will of the German armies to continue to resist. Rose saw action at the most important battles of the Great War including Ypres, the Somme and Cambrai. This account of the battery in action on the Somme is one of the most important primary source accounts of the day to day experiences of a British field battery which saw service in the latter stages of the battle.

This exceptionally well written and detailed account deepens our understanding of the reality of what it meant to be involved in this terrifying conflict and fills a gap in the literature of the Great War by bringing the lives of the artillerymen on the Somme into focus.

A CONSIDERABLE NUMBER OF HOSTILE 'Minnies' made conditions somewhat unpleasant for the infantry in the trenches, and during the night the battery position was subjected to indirect machine-gun fire, which necessitated a certain amount of caution in moving about. The O.P.'s were well placed, and afforded us an excellent view, for we overlooked the enemy's lines, and could see some distance beyond them. We were now on the fringe of the battle, and away half right, on clear days, we could see the struggle progressing, as a considerable dent had already been made. The sight was a very grand one, especially after dark. The Verey Lights and various S.O.S. rockets, which were frequently sent up by our opponents, made a fine spectacular display, far finer than any firework exhibition we had ever witnessed in our own country in prewar days.

Gradually the Division was side-slipped to the south, and our next position was close to the station of Mailly. We did not remain there long, however, as the time had now arrived for us to put in an appearance in the battle itself. We spent one night close to Amiens, and availed ourselves of the opportunity to hold a dinner there, which was attended by all the original officers in the Brigade - a last night of fun and merriment before the long, stiff fight ahead of us, for who knew how many would survive the ordeal. The next day brought us to Vaux, on the River Somme, and, in the first week in September, we found ourselves immersed in the battle. We took up our first position in the lately captured second line German system, facing Montauban and covering Guillemont, which had just been taken by an Irish Division.

Very stiff fighting was in progress on this sector, as we were now nearing the summit of the Ridge, the possession of which would be invaluable, as the enemy's territory would be laid bare to us, and he would lose his observation over us. It was not surprising, therefore, that he fought with the courage of despair and initiated counter-attack upon counter-attack, all of which we had to meet with great determination. The weather was extremely hot, which added much to the discomfort; and, as progress had been very slow for some time, it was impossible to clear up the battlefield, and the stench was almost insupportable. At length the village of Ginchy was captured, and, with our men installed on the further side of the slope, the fighting for position came to an end. We were now entering on the third stage of the great battle, which had commenced more than two months previously. An attack, on a large scale, was planned, the object being to drive the enemy down the slope of the hill into the low-lying country beyond. Field batteries were moved up into forward positions, in order to assist the infantry, by placing a creeping barrage - a new and most successful invention, afterwards employed on all occasions - in front of the advancing waves of men: and the "heavies", of which, for the first time, we possessed a preponderance, pounded the enemy communications far behind his lines.

The assault was delivered over a wide area, early in the morning of the 15th of September, but in no way did it come up to expectations - in fact, it might almost be counted a reverse. Some divisions did well, and took their objectives, but others were completely held up, at certain strong points, which necessitated the withdrawal of the remainder, in order to keep the line uniform. The Guards met with instant success, and took their final objectives, only to discover that the Division on each side of them had made little progress and could get no further. They were reluctantly forced to return, and it was while doing so that heavy casualties were inflicted on them, as they were raked with fire from the sides as well as in front. During the withdrawal, a party of machine-gunners occupied a trench, and attempted to screen the retirement of the main body of troops, by holding the enemy at bay. In order to use this machine-gun to the best advantage, the piece was placed on top of the parapet, exposed to the full view of the oncoming hordes, but our men never wavered in serving it, and, as soon as one gunner dropped at his post, another instantly took the vacant place, although it meant certain death within a few moments.

Next day they were pulled out to refit, and, as they marched back to rest, a very touching sight was witnessed. A certain battalion, a mere remnant, swung along, headed by its band. All the officers had become casualties, and the Battalion Sergeant-Major was in command, but as many of the dead officers as could be recovered were brought back on stretchers and placed each in his proper position. Headed by the body of their late Commander, the column proceeded on its way, the men marching at attention, and, although covered with mud and blood-stained, they might have been proceeding down the Mall. Such is the discipline of the Guards, and every tribute of respect was paid them by the troops through whom they passed.

The next battle was timed for the 25th inst., and our infantry came back to the line a couple of days before that date. There was much suppressed excitement and curiosity, for the mysterious Tanks were to participate on this occasion for the first time, and it was thought that the secret had been so well kept that the would come as a complete surprise to the enemy. This proved to be the case, and the attack was a great success. What was known as the Flers line was everywhere penetrated, and all gains were held. The Tanks did splendid work. They advanced well ahead of the infantry, and battered down barbed wire, overran trenches, smashed machine-gun emplacements, killing the gun crews, and even waddled as far as the village of Gueudecourt. There they effected much execution and caused great panic among the enemy reserves, which were concentrating for the inevitable counter attack.

Thus the battle continued, sometimes breaking out into fierce fights and at other times reduced to isolated scraps, but all the time the enemy was being gradually and relentlessly pushed down into the valley, and the villages of Morval, Les Boeufs, and Gueudecourt fell into our hands.

It was almost uncanny the way in which villages would completely disappear. For instance, at the time when these hamlets first came within our vision, on our reaching the crest of the hill, they appeared almost intact, but a few days rendered them unrecognisable - they had become merely so many heaps of rubble. There are many places on the Somme which have literally not one brick standing on top of another, and one would never imagine for a moment that a prosperous little village had ever existed there.

Many changes of battery positions were made, and, whenever possible, we burrowed down into the ground, as the enemy's heavy pieces were out after our blood. The great concentration of guns and the few suitable localities for placing them in action added to our difficulties, and we were thus rendered an easy target for the hostile counter batteries. Innumerable brigades were huddled close together, in what was known as the Death Valley, for the simple reason that there was no other suitable spot wherein to place them, and heavy casualties resulted. We had the good fortune, however, to be somewhat isolated from the others, and occupied a forward position, where the guns were hidden in an old German communication trench. The enemy never found it, but subjected us, now and again, to a general burst of harassing fire: his main volume of hate passed us by far overhead.

And, meanwhile, what of our friend the F.O.O.? In those days his lot was by no means an enviable one, and it was a task of no mean magnitude to keep communications going between the trenches and the guns. However, it had to be done, or at least attempted, and the following is a brief account of a typical day in the life of a gunner subaltern.

Orders would be given that a certain hostile trench was to be subjected to a severe, annihilating bombardment, and this necessitated the laying out of a wire to a part of our front line, from which the shoot could be registered, as the target could not be observed from any other locality than the trench immediately opposite it. The F.O.O. rises early in the morning, and sets out with his little squad of telephonists and linesmen. He requires to post a signalman and linesman at frequent intervals, called Relay Stations, in order to preserve communication, as the wire is being continually broken by hostile gun-fire. Progress, in a case like this, is necessarily slow, and he has to pick his way among the shell-holes, seeking as much protection, for the line, as circumstances will permit. The signallers follow in his foot steps, staggering along under the weight of a large reel of wire. All goes well until they reach the summit of a ridge, when, suddenly, a barrage from a "whizz bang" battery is placed right down on top of the party. There is nothing for it but to remain crouched in a friendly shell-hole, which affords a little protection, until the storm blows over or to risk the chances of being hit in the open. The journey is then resumed, and much relief is felt when at last the ground over a nasty dip is traversed without mishap, as this is known to be a favourite target for hostile gunners. A muddy, unkempt communication-trench is now entered, and the party proceed, up a slope, towards the support system, and eventually arrive at their destination - a post in the front line overlooking its objective. Difficulty is experienced in preserving the wire from the unguarded feet of infantrymen, who look askance at the party as it passes, cursing the idiosyncrasies of each fire bay. The instrument is connected with the end of the wire, and all hold their breath in order to hear the answering buzz which tells them that they are through to the battery. Several futile buzzes may be made by the telephonist, and then, no response being forth coming, a linesman is sent down the wire towards the first relay station. A break in the wire is discovered and speedily mended, the next attempt is successful, and the battery is called to action.

During registration the wire often breaks, and serious delays occur, but, at length, the last gun is duly pronounced O.K. by the officer. Just in the nick of time, too! For the enemy commences a sharp retaliation on the portion of the trench occupied by the little party. Refuge is sought in an old enemy shaft close lay, and there it awaits the lime for the "show" to commence. Several other batteries also take part in the shoot, and it is quite impossible to pick out the shells which belong to each one as they fall. Complete success crowns the effort, but on the particular day here described the F.O.O. and party failed to see the end of the bout, as they were subjected to very heavy fire, and were all blown down the mouth of the shaft by the explosion of a shell. Luckily, though badly shaken, all escaped without injury.

Meanwhile the wire has been broken in many places and is beyond repair, but it has already served its purpose, and, when fire has died down, the party starts on the return journey. On arriving at the first relay station, the telephonist on duty is found dead at his post, the receiver still clutched in his hand and held to his ear. A nasty gash in the forehead reveals the place where he has been hit and instantly killed. His companion is nowhere to be found, although bloodstains denote that he has at least been wounded, and, on investigation, it is ascertained that the linesman has been hit, picked up by passing comrades, and taken to an aid-post. The journey is resumed, the party carrying the dead with them, and presently another hostile barrage is encountered. Again the men lie low until it ceases, and then pick up the remaining linesmen, and return to the battery utterly exhausted. Many questions are asked, and it frequently happens that the F.O.O. is cursed by his Battery Commander for not keeping the wire going, and even the Brigade joins in the chorus. The young officer pays little heed, and inwardly reflects that they should be extremely thankful that communication was established at all, and that those of the party who returned did so in safety. So, in spite of everything, he consumes a hearty dinner and retires to bed, sleeping the sleep of the just, and soon becomes oblivious of all his little worries and sombre surroundings.

Towards the middle of October the weather broke, and conditions became intolerable. The roads, which had been partially repaired, were still soft and broken, and developed into quagmires - mud and water to a depth of two and three feet made vehicular traffic almost out of the question. All ammunition had to be transported to the guns by means of horses carrying pack saddles, a slow and tedious method, which took a lot out of men and beasts alike. As yet no decca-ville railways had been constructed as far as battery positions. Very heavy work thus fell on those at the wagon lines, who were kept busy most of the day and night. Although the distance to the gun position was under five miles there and back, the journey rarely took less than ten hours to accomplish. If a horse fell down in this sticky mud, heavily laden as it was, attempts at rescue proved unavailing, except on rare occasions, even with the aid of drag-ropes, and the unfortunate animal had to be "dispatched." Was it a sense of humour that prompted those in authority to send the subalterns, in turn, to the wagon lines for a "rest"? Anyhow, it was considered anything but that by the poor unfortunates who went, and right glad they were when the time came round for their next period of duty with the guns!

As the weather rapidly became worse, operations came to a standstill, and all proceeded to dig themselves in for the coming winter. Every endeavour was made to make our quarters water-proof, as well as shell-proof, and some attempts at mining were commenced, but the condition of the ground was all against such an undertaking, and the work was abandoned. Then whispers spread abroad that we were to be relieved for a short rest, and, after ten weeks of incessant fighting, we were withdrawn from the line and marched to a little village named Hangest, a few miles west of Amiens. There we were glad to find ourselves installed in billets with a root covering us once more. A week of leisure helped greatly to restore our spirits, and again we set out for the line. Our destination this time was Combles, and we took over a battery position from the French, who politely made us acquainted with our new surroundings. Our allies, who had been fighting side-by-side with us on our right flank throughout the great battle, were then withdrawn, and the British front was extended to the south as far as the banks of the River Somme. Evidence was speedily forthcoming to convince us of the severe nature of the recent fight. The ground was strewn with wreckage and material of all descriptions, and many hostile guns were found abandoned or lying where they had been put out of action by the irresistible dash of the Poilus.

The country, in this part, was undulating, and better suited to the concealment of battery positions, and nowhere was the enemy able to overlook our territory. Our area included the defence of the joint villages of Sailly-Saillisel, situated on commanding ground, which the French had recently bravely stormed. Combles, too, which lay in a basin shaped hollow, was interesting as having been the centre of supplies for the southern portion of the German Army operating in the battle, and much booty was discovered in the huge catacombs which ran underneath the town.

'Xmas passed in much the same way as in the previous year. A smart bombardment was carried out in the morning in order to advise the enemy that anything in the way of fraternising would not be countenanced by us. At mid-day the men partook of their 'Xmas fare, which had been fetched from Amiens, and a short service was conducted by the Padre in one of the gun-pits. A slight disturbance took place at dusk, when the

S.O.S. went up from the front line and all bitteries immediately opened out. It seemed a rather extraordinary occurrence, as the evening was unusually quiet, and, presently, it was discovered to have arisen through an error, due to the fact that the enemy had put up a coloured light in between two ordinary Verey lights which constituted our own S.O.S.

About this time the enemy caused considerable annoyance to a certain Battalion Headquarters, situated in a quarry close behind the lines, by occasionally dropping a shell right into it, the position having probably been discovered by his aircraft. Retaliation tactics were adopted, which consisted of subjecting the hostile trenches to a sharp half-hour's bombardment from eight batteries, firing a total of 2,000 rounds The enemy was well known to be very thick-skinned, but these measures met with instant success, and it was only necessary to remind him once again that we were not to be trifled with in this way.

After the New Year, a severe spell of frost set in, with an occasional heavy fall of snow, and we were somewhat annoyed when orders came through to sideslip our position further south, as we had made our quarters fairly comfortable by this time, and expected to remain undisturbed throughout the winter. The new position was situated behind the ruined village of Rancourt, facing St Pierre Yaast wood, and was one of the worst and most disagreeable localities it was ever our lot to occupy, as we were, more or less, water-logged the whole of our time there. Much difficulty was experienced by both friend and foe in entering their respective front line, so much so that, by common consent, sniping by rifle fire was discontinued until parapets were constructed and made fit for occupation. However, sniping was still indulged in by the artillery, and no parties of any size were permitted to go about freely near the front line under observation. Affairs continued thus until the middle of February, when it became apparent that something unusual was taking place in enemy territory, and great explosions were heard, after which volumes of smoke were seen to rise in large columns. These, as was afterwards proved, were due to preparations being made by the enemy to evacuate the low-lying country, into which they had reluctantly been forced, as the result of the Battle of the Somme, prior to falling back upon the great prepared defences known as the Hindenburg Line.

Instantly everyone was on the alert for further signs of evacuation, and one morning a patrol reported that the enemy had vacated their front line. Further patrols were at once pushed out, through St. Pierre Vaast wood, in order to maintain contact with the retreating foe. Every precaution had to be taken, as it was soon discovered that many forms of booby-traps had been cunningly laid by him in his wake, and progress was necessarily slow. Added to this, there was great difficulty in manoeuvring the guns over the innumerable trenches which existed in the neighbourhood, and the pieces sank up to their axles in the clogging mud, and were only extricated after hours of labour. The enemy retired slowly and most methodically, destroying everything of value and wantonly reducing the small villages and hamlets to mere shells, by means of incendiary bombs. The inhabitants also were removed beforehand, and, when the troops advanced, they might have been traversing a wilderness, so complete was the ruin and desolation on all sides.

The time had now arrived for the Brigade to have a much-needed rest and also to refit, so, at the end of March, we were withdrawn from the contest. Marching westward, we arrived at the village of Morlancourt in the first week of April, well content at the prospect of returning to civilization for a protracted period.

- CHAPTER 7 -

LETTERS FROM
A SOLDIER

by Isaac Alexander Mack

THE LETTERS OF ISAAC ALEXANDER MACK who fell on the first day of the Somme while commanding his trench mortar battery make for particularly poignant reading. The jaunty almost Woosterish tone of the letters complete with the copious use of the phrase 'topping' to describe anything which the writer viewed in a positive light makes these letters all the more heart rending. This is especially true when we consider this care-free young man is about to have his life taken away from him. After his death the letters were collected and published privately as a lasting memorial to 'Alex' in a slim volume entitled *Letters from a Soldier*.

* * * * *

AT 11 P.M. I WENT UP TO THE TRENCHES with Carroll and half the Battery, who were going in for the night - the men in one big dug-out and Carroll in one with two machine gunners. I returned home and got to bed about 3 A.M.

The next morning I was wakened before seven by the guns waking up for their early morning hate just under my window. There are Batteries dotted about all over the place here 18 pounders, howitzers of all sizes, and naval guns. You almost trip over them wherever you go. There are two 6 in. howitzers hiding in our back garden. I went up to the trenches to look round the next morning (Monday).

The trenches here are very different from what we have been used to, they are long narrow trenches, not breastworks, dug down in the chalk, a veritable labyrinth of trenches, going in all directions, up-hill and down dale. They are very deep, and very few rifle shots are fired. Sniping is done with field guns and trench mortars. The line is very curious, moving forward and backward. In one place in our line a village runs out and there is a German salient. In front of the salient lots of mines have been exploded and no trenches remain, merely holes that bombers hide in, where the trench bulges in again we share our parapet with the Bosche. I don't go there often, as you have to crawl, and you usually crawl into the wrong trench and find yourselves wandering in the Bosche lines. The Germans send over a lot of oil cans filled with old razor blades and rubbish, which do a good deal of damage, and are rather unpleasant. However, we are educating them not to send them over too often, as we send over two to their one with our mortars, and in time we shall get them under our thumbs I hope. We always have one man by each gun firing almost continuously. We have dug-outs well back with wire beds in them, also rats! Here we have big underground dug-outs 20 feet underground, some of them down long stairways. The country is very hilly and wooded in parts; our part of the line has two hills and one valley, it is rather like Salisbury Plain, or a flat edition of Derbyshire.

Carroll has been in, and I have gone up in the daytime.

I am going to relieve him this afternoon; I shall only be in a few days. I hope to come home on leave about June 4th.

Much love to all, from your loving Son,

ALEC.

P.S. - I have not got your letter, but I have received all the letters and things sent, I think.

* * * * *

My darling Mother, -

I am writing this in my dug-out. It seems very comfortable at present. We have one large dug-out in which Carroll slept with two machine gunners. I was going to sleep there too, and as I have a new officer, Ingle, with me he was going to sleep there. But by the greatest stroke of good fortune I spotted this one just near. It is the best dug-out I have ever had. The other dug-out is swarming with mice and rats, who scratch earth into you all the time, and come and expire on you at night. One fell down and died on the table while we were having tea. But in this I have only seen one mouse so far, and it has got about ten feet of solid earth over it. I sleep on a comfortable folding bed, in my clothes, of course. It is well back six or seven hundred yards from the firing line. The firing line is more unhealthy than other trenches we have been in. They will keep sending the oil cans I told you of over into the front line. If you manage to get away from them round a traverse they come rolling round the corner after you; I don't love them at all. I have got "Printer's Pie," and I am just going to put up some pictures and am then going to bed. I relieved Carroll, and have been messing around since. I went down to the firing line for an hour or two to go to each emplacement and see how the men who were firing the guns were getting on, and then came back and observed their fire just outside my dug-out; there is our observation post from which you can see our own lines and the Bosche lines for miles. I have just been down to one of our ammunition dug-outs, seeing 100 rounds put in that a fatigue party had brought up. Friday 10 to 12. Good-night, Mother mine.

Had a comfortable night, but, as it was rather cold, I have had my sleeping bag brought up for to-night, so I shall be all right. Fuller was late this morning, so I had to wait impatiently for my boots and puttees to be cleaned before I could get up, consequently we did not have breakfast till nearly 10 o'clock. After breakfast Ingle and I went round all our emplacements. We had quite an interesting time, as in one place where the trench is not occupied, and up which we have to go to one emplacement, one of our field gun batteries put four shots into the trench about 10 yards behind Ingle and knocked him over, then a rifle grenade landed nearly at my feet and kindly failed to go off. We returned in time for a late scrappy lunch at 2.30. When I was intending to have a nap and a read when one of the Northumberland Fusiliers officers, Bowkett, turned up with Kitty to see the line, as he is probably taking it over from us in a few days, and I had to wander right around all the emplacements again. After tea I went down to see how our guns were getting on and found the infantry were very pleased with them, as one gun had managed to destroy a Hun machine gun emplacement, and the others must have done considerable damage, as they so much raised the Hun's ire that he shelled them all unsuccessfully.

We had a pleasant dinner, and the rest of the evening I have spent worrying over returns, new emplacements, trench maps, etc, and so to a well-earned rest.

I am beginning to find my way about a bit now, but there is a veritable maze of nice white chalk trenches. We are in a sort of valley, and in the middle of the valley is a slight rise on which the village of La Boiselle once existed, and which now forms the German salient.

Sunday, 28th, 1 A.M. Wakened up by Parker, of the Lincolns to tell me that gas cylinders have been seen being taken in La Boiselle, and that, as the wind is in the right direction, there may be a gas attack. I hope not; however put on boots and puttees. I warned the men, putting one sentry on duty, as also the servants. I have a beastly headache, and I am very tired; I wish people wouldn't see such things. They are very quiet, too, to-night, which looks suspicious.

May 29th. Awakened very tired about 8 o'clock, dressed by putting on my boots, sponge bath, shaved while I had my breakfast in my dug-out. Then I went with my sergeant to see about new emplacements. Started on a new one with a corporal and four men working, also myself. In the afternoon I received a scheme for construction of six new emplacements, and I had to go to try and find positions. I managed more or less to do so, and returned in time to start working out ranges, compass bearing, angles, &c., only to find I had to go down to two emplacements again to place them accurately by the map. Busy all evening with indents, returns and chiefly with schemes for emplacements. Bed at last - 12 midnight.

Yesterday we worked on emplacements till about 2, when I returned for lunch, and was strafed by the Divisional General for having my guns in the firing line; afterwards a disturbed lunch, during which we were shelled and our men's dug-out pushed in with a 5.9 howitzer, though 16 men in the dug-out were unhurt. The Bosche was busy all day with 5.9's, blowing most things in. In the afternoon I went up to see the Brigadier, who was very nice, and attempted to solve all my difficulties. I then had dinner with Carroll and Brand, and returned to the trenches, and so to bed.

This morning I wakened at 7.30 Tempest came in, laying claims to my dug-out, claiming it for Barker, but we said "No." Breakfast at 8. At 9 I prospected with Wilson-Jones and found a topping place for a new emplacement, which we set up forthwith, also making on the other two new ones. Lake and another man came to lunch. This afternoon and evening we have been doing more work on the emplacements. I am getting a bit tired of these trenches; they are much too dangerous, and I hate suddenly having to crouch against a traverse when a big shell comes and crouches on the other side of it. I shall now retire to my little couch. Good-night, Mother dear.

June 1st. Working all day on emplacements, putting headcover on, &c. This evening, about six o'clock, I was called upon to reply to German trench mortars, but just as we had reached the bottom of the communication, they opened gun fire on the communication trench, wounding several men, while we lay at the bottom of the trench, while they whizzed over in sort of sheets of shells. They soon quieted, but one burst was enough. I went down to the front line about 10 to look round, and coming back they were unpleasant again - big stuff too - but to our left. The shells are something terrific here; I think it is one of the hottest parts of the line.

June 2nd. Working all day on emplacements. In the evening we were called upon to retaliate for German mortars, and pumped hell into them for a few minutes (excuse the word, it is the only one I can think of), and soon shut them up. I was relieved by Carroll.

June 3rd. Went up to the trenches, to see how the emplacements were getting on, with Kitty. In the evening the Tyneside Scottish relieved us, going up to the trenches at 2 A.M. instead of 2 P.M. We had an awful crush of them in our mess for several hours, and I had great difficulty in pushing them off up to the trenches. I took them there just to be in time for a terrific bombardment on the trenches, whilst the Germans tried unsuccessfully to raid our trenches. They used tear gas on us, sent over in shells, and it makes you weep. When I returned they were shelling near our billet, and we had to spend the whole of the rest of the night in the cellars, and only got to our bed at about 6 in the morning.

June 4th. Carroll and Brand went back to rest with the two new batteries, and Kitty and I remained in reserve, as they wanted us to take part in a raid that we were going to do, and, though our own brigade was in rest, our batteries were selected as a compliment to take part in the raid, which we learned was to come off on Monday, June 5th, so we tried to go to bed early on Sunday after our troublous Saturday night. However, we learnt that the division on our right was doing a raid, and the Bosche started retaliating on Albert, the town we were in, so we had to spend another night in the cellars.

June 5th. We spent the day getting ammunition up, 400 rounds, registering our guns, &c. We found our emplacements damaged by the bombardment of the night before and had to make one new one. We meant to return to our billet for lunch at 2 P.M., but we actually came back at 6 - in time for high tea. At 8.30 P.M. we paraded, six men from each battery to work four guns, and got to the trenches to find everything quiet. We prepared our ammunition, &c., and were finished just before 11 P.M., at which time all our artillery suddenly burst forth into a hundred thunderstorms, and absolutely rained shells on the German lines like hail. At 11.20 P.M. we started, and put over about 70 rounds from each gun, and finished at 11.35 P.M., and returned to the third line as soon as possible to collect there to take our guns out. I quite enjoyed it all; there was a huge row on, and you could not tell if any German shells were coming at you, there was such a noise. It was quite exciting. I was surprised to find that it is really not nearly half so bad when both sides are hard at it and our own getting decidedly the best of it, as when occasional shots keep arriving.

We were glad to get out all right at 1.30 and back to our billet. The next day (Tuesday) we moved back to Bresle, and arrived there in the evening. Kitty and I had to go up to the trenches to collect some things, then we had tea, and came along in motor wagons, &c.

At present we are back where we were in tents; it rains fairly often, and, as a rest, we have to parade at 6.45 A.M. for field days. I am going to the Suffolks to-night.

I am awfully sorry this letter has been so long, but I have been made O.C. group of four batteries, and I have had to work all day and most of the night.

I am very fit and well, and hope to be home on June 15th. Old Wroxan, who shared a room with me at Cambridge, was killed the other day - he had only been out about a month.

Socks, cake and all sorts of nice things received.

Much love to all, from your loving Son,

ALEC.

*   *   *   *   *

B.E.F., 10th.

My darling Mother, -

As I told you in my last letter we are now resting, and we are doing it very vigorously indeed. There are two kinds of rest for Infantry in the British Army, and they are (1) A good rest, and (2) a thoroughly good rest. A good rest is when your brigade is in the trenches, and your battalion or unit is out. Then between shells in the trenches you rest. You begin the cure at 7 in the morning, if you are lucky, and continue it all day and all night on working parties.

When you are having a thoroughly good rest you rise at 6 A.M., parade at 6.45 A.M. every day, and charge across country, practicing the assault for the day that has always been coming (is always in a fortnight) and never comes off - the great Spring Offensive. That's what we have been doing the last few days, walking five or six miles out, then walking two miles or so across country, and then marching home. Every day we receive orders in the afternoon that the brigade will go somewhere, to the trenches or to some other village, but they are always cancelled in the evening.

Fortunately, to-morrow is Sunday, and we are to have a day's rest. I hope it will not be cancelled.

Last night I had dinner with "C" Company, my old Company; we had a wonderful dinner. This evening we went to our brigade theatre. It is an old barn, and we all sit on the floor - Colonels, Majors, Subalterns and privates. There are cinematograph films, songs, &c., and it is very cheering; Kitty, Dougal and I went together to-night. The chief talk is all about leave, everyone being in hopes of it, and all except the staff being put off from week to week until you almost despair of it. Dougal is just talking about hopping into a big hot bath and a feather bed, but if we had never done without them we should not value them quite as we do now.

Wednesday, 14th. The Day of Days, the heaven of every British soldier. Leave, that Will-o'-the-Wisp which everyone possesses, but which evades all but the staff, and the very lucky. A long journey from Mericourt, starting at 9.30 to Havre. Lunch off omelette and coffee during an hour's halt in the dignified perambulations of a French train at Bouchie. At Havre we rushed to get cabins, but found plenty, and we soon went to bed - Payne and I (Bernard Thompson on the same boat) - and we slept until wakened one hour out of Southampton. Breakfast off a cup of coffee, and then train again.

Winnie met me at Waterloo, or rather I met her, gazing forlornly at streams of strange soldiers. All morning at Harold's offices and shopping, lunching at the Criterion, &c. Then on to Win's to tea and back in bare time to the Savoy to change for dinner. Then to "To-night's the night" - topping seats and a good show.

*   *   *   *   *

The writer of these letters arrived in England June 15th, 1916, and returned to France June 22nd. The Spring Offensive, of which he wrote, was launched at 7.30 on July 1ˢᵗ, 1916, and on that day he was killed near La Boiselle - "A corner of a foreign field that is for ever England."

Writing of him a fellow Officer said:-

"The last time I saw him was on Friday afternoon, June 30ᵗʰ, in the cellars of the Château. He was gaily talking to his Officers and giving them one or two final instructions. 'Have some tea of dog biscuits and bully beef' he said to me just as I had finished a wash. I said 'Good-bye' to him, and then crept along the dark passage to the Château.

He was one of the real enthusiasts for war amongst us as a regiment. Most people had joined because it was their duty - he joined because he was a soldier by nature as well. If there was to be a scrap he was sure to be in it. He wanted to go out before the battalion on July 1ˢᵗ, but the C.O., of course, would not hear of it.

At Armentières I was told that when the Corner Fort was bombarded he was hit on his helmet by a huge piece of shell, but just carried on. I feel certain he died in the forefront of the battle, for his pluck was proverbial. "Whoever else gets the wind up - Mack won't" I heard an Officer of the regiment say one day during a bad spell in the trenches.

I do not believe he was afraid of death, and I am sure he fell as far forward as the German leaden hail would let anyone get alive."

Another one wrote:-

"I saw a good deal of him during the last few days before July 1ˢᵗ, as his battery was encamped with us. He was in the highest spirits, though he knew he was to occupy a most exposed position in the attack.

He was as brave as any man I know, and his loss is tremendous. I, as well as all his friends out here, sympathise most deeply with his family, whose consolation must be that he died a gallant soldier's death."